The Crying of Lot 49 is widely recognized as a significant contemporary work which frames the desire for meaning and the quest for knowledge within the social and political contexts of the 1950s and 1960s in the U.S. In the introduction to this collection of original essays on Thomas Pynchon's important novel, Patrick O'Donnell discusses the background and critical reception of the novel. Further essays by five experts on contemporary literature examine the novel's "semiotic regime" or the way in which it organizes signs; the comparison of postmodernist Pynchon and the influential South American writer Jorge Luis Borges; metaphor in the novel; the novel's narrative strategies; and the novel within the cultural contexts of American Puritanism and the Beat movement. Together, these essays provide an examination of *The Crying of Lot 49* within its literary, historical, and scientific contexts.

NEW ESSAYS ON THE CRYING OF LOT 49

★ The American Novel ★

GENERAL EDITOR

Emory Elliott
University of California, Riverside

Other books in the series:
New Essays on The Scarlet Letter
New Essays on The Great Gatsby
New Essays on Adventures of Huckleberry Finn
New Essays on Moby-Dick
New Essays on Uncle Tom's Cabin
New Essays on The Red Badge of Courage
New Essays on The Sun Also Rises
New Essays on The American
New Essays on Light in August
New Essays on Invisible Man
New Essays on The Awakening
New Essays on The Portrait of a Lady
New Essays on Native Son
New Essays on The Grapes of Wrath
New Essays on A Farewell to Arms
New Essays on Winesburg, Ohio
New Essays on Their Eyes Were Watching God
New Essays on The Rise of Silas Lapham
New Essays on Sister Carrie
New Essays on White Noise

New Essays on
The Crying of Lot 49

Edited by
Patrick O'Donnell

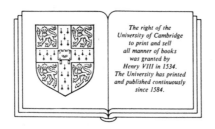

The right of the
University of Cambridge
to print and sell
all manner of books
was granted by
Henry VIII in 1534.
The University has printed
and published continuously
since 1584.

CAMBRIDGE UNIVERSITY PRESS

Cambridge

New York Port Chester Melbourne Sydney

Published by the Press Syndicate of the University of Cambridge
The Pitt Building, Trumpington Street, Cambridge CB2 1RP
40 West 20th Street, New York, NY 10011, USA
10 Stamford Road, Oakleigh, Melbourne 3166, Australia

First published 1991

Printed in the United States of America

Library of Congress Cataloging-in-Publication Data

New essays on The crying of lot 49 / edited by Patrick O'Donnell.
    p.   cm. — (The American novel)
Includes bibliographical references.
ISBN 0-521-38163-0. — ISBN 0-521-38833-3 (pbk.)
1. Pynchon, Thomas. Crying of lot 49.   I. O'Donnell, Patrick,
            1948–   .   II. Series.
            PS3566.Y55C796   1991
        813'.54 – dc20   91-18935

A catalogue record for this book is available from the British Library.

ISBN 0–521–38163–0 hardback
ISBN 0–521–38833–3 paperback

Contents

Series Editor's Preface
page vii

1
Introduction
PATRICK O'DONNELL
page 1

2
Borges and Pynchon:
The Tenuous Symmetries of Art
DEBRA A. CASTILLO
page 21

3
Toward the Schizo-Text: Paranoia as
Semiotic Regime in *The Crying of Lot 49*
JOHN JOHNSTON
page 47

4
"Hushing Sick Transmissions":
Disrupting Story in *The Crying of Lot 49*
BERNARD DUYFHUIZEN
page 79

Contents

5

"A Metaphor of God Knew How Many Parts":
The Engine that Drives *The Crying of Lot 49*
N. KATHERINE HAYLES
page 97

6
A Re-cognition of Her
Errand into the Wilderness
PIERRE-YVES PETILLON
page 127

Notes on Contributors
page 171

Selected Bibliography
page 173

Series Editor's Preface

In literary criticism the last twenty-five years have been particularly fruitful. Since the rise of the New Criticism in the 1950s, which focused attention of critics and readers upon the text itself – apart from history, biography, and society – there has emerged a wide variety of critical methods which have brought to literary works a rich diversity of perspectives: social, historical, political, psychological, economic, ideological, and philosophical. While attention to the text itself, as taught by the New Critics, remains at the core of contemporary interpretation, the widely shared assumption that works of art generate many different kinds of interpretation has opened up possibilities for new readings and new meanings.

Before this critical revolution, many American novels had come to be taken for granted by earlier generations of readers as having an established set of recognized interpretations. There was a sense among many students that the canon was established and that the larger thematic and interpretative issues had been decided. The task of the new reader was to examine the ways in which elements such as structure, style, and imagery contributed to each novel's acknowledged purpose. But recent criticism has brought these old assumptions into question and has thereby generated a wide variety of original, and often quite surprising, interpretations of the classics, as well as of rediscovered novels such at Kate Chopin's *The Awakening,* which has only recently entered the canon of works that scholars and critics study and that teachers assign their students.

The aim of The American Novel Series is to provide students of American literature and culture with introductory critical guides to

American novels now widely read and studied. Each volume is devoted to a single novel and begins with an introduction by the volume editor, a distinguished authority on the text. The introduction presents details of the novel's composition, publication, history, and contemporary reception, as well as a survey of the major critical trends and readings from first publication to the present. This overview is followed by four or five original essays, specifically commissioned from senior scholars of established reputation and from outstanding younger critics. Each essay presents a distinct point of view, and together they constitute a forum of interpretative methods and of the best contemporary ideas on each text.

It is our hope that these volumes will convey the vitality of current critical work in American literature, generate new insights and excitement for students of the American novel, and inspire new respect for and new perspectives upon these major literary texts.

Emory Elliott
University of California, Riverside

1

Introduction

PATRICK O'DONNELL

THOMAS Pynchon's second novel, *The Crying of Lot 49*, was published in 1966; that same year, the Manila Summit on America's increasing involvement in Vietnam took place, "Hogan's Heroes," "Green Acres," and "Gomer Pyle, U.S.M.C." were top-rated television situation comedies, and *Esquire* published an article entitled "Wake Up America, It Can't Happen Here: A Post-McCarthy Guide to Twenty-Three Conspiracies by Assorted Enemies Within."[1] Such is the contemporary cultural context out of which Pynchon's enigmatic, conspiracy-ridden novel emerged – a novel which, in many ways, easily seduces us into linking an article in a popular magazine, television programs, and an historical event to the fortunes of a fictional character named Oedipa Maas. But it would be a mistake to assume that there is any definitive connection to be made between "fiction" and "history" by comparing the novel – in its moment of production – to the selected particularities of its cultural milieux. For *The Crying of Lot 49* speculates upon the whole idea of "connection," or the activity of connecting, as *the* characteristic human endeavor, whether it be in writing and reading literary works, or in articulating ourselves – our identities – as historical beings. We *need* to narrate, Pynchon's novel argues; we feel the necessity to create and perceive significant patterns in all that we read and do; we are driven to see the connections between the events of our own lives and the larger, external events of that unfolding story we call "history." However, in the familiar dilemma posed in all of Pynchon's novels, but never so dramatically as in *The Crying of Lot 49*, this need to make sense and perceive patterns of significance in text, life, and history can easily become the activity of the para-

1

noid, who is poised between the fear that, in the end, nothing makes sense and the desire to see plots, connections, significance everywhere.

Chaos or totalitarian order; meaninglessness or paranoia; void or dark design – these are the polarities of Thomas Pynchon's *oeuvre,* which in 1991 numbers four novels, several short stories, and a scattering of essays and reviews. With the publication of *V.* in 1963, Pynchon arose almost immediately as a major postwar writer who had tapped into the fantasies and fears of a generation just emerging from the McCarthy era and about to embark upon a long nightmare of presidential assassinations, social violence, and the Vietnam War. *V.* garnered a number of laudatory reviews upon its appearance and won the prestigious Faulkner Foundation award for the best first novel of 1963. This labyrinthine assemblage of puzzles, plots, and counterplots immediately brought to its author a public recognition which has grown with the appearance of each succeeding novel, and which Pynchon has successfully parried (and, perhaps unintentionally, nourished) with his notorious reclusiveness – matched only in the annals of contemporary American literature by that of J. D. Salinger.[2] The details of Pynchon's biography are, accordingly, sparse, and one might well have the paranoid sense that, given the control the author has maintained over the projection of his public image (or lack of it), the few available details that do exist are only the ones Pynchon has allowed to leak out or those of little consequence. But their very scarcity has made them of special interest to many of Pynchon's readers, who search in vain for any straightforward manifestation of the autobiographical presence of the author in his fiction. Recognizing, then, as Peggy Kamuf argues, that "[b]iographical narrative appears . . . to be the most economical means of gathering, with some semblance of coherence, the disparate marks left by the practice of writing," we offer these scattered facts about Pynchon's life in order to place his work – a work most clearly concerned with the limits of writing and the illusory, dangerous power of coherent plots – within the useful, but partial and suspect, framework of Pynchon's "biography."[3]

Thomas Pynchon was born on May 8, 1937, and grew up in the middle-class suburbs of Long Island.[4] His earliest authorial efforts are recorded in his frequent contributions to the Oyster Bay *Purple and Gold,* his high school newspaper, most notably in a column entitled "The Voice of the Hamster" written under various pseudonyms: "Boscoe Stein," "Roscoe Stein," and "Bosc." Pynchon graduated from high school in 1953, began his university studies at Cornell University as an engineering physics major, interrupted his college career with a two-year tour of duty in the Navy, apparently serving as a signal corpsman, then completed his studies at Cornell (where he took a class from Vladimir Nabokov), earning a B.A. degree in English. Pynchon began writing stories during his undergraduate days (his first two, "The Small Rain" and "Mortality and Mercy in Vienna," were published in 1959) and worked on the campus literary journal with Richard Fariña, who wrote about Pynchon in his series of reminiscences about the late 1950s and early 1960s, *Long Time Coming and a Long Time Gone.*[5] In a satirical remembrance Fariña recalls Pynchon as being lanky, taciturn, and in search of tacos after a brief absence from Mexico, where he lived for much of the early 1960s.[6] Pynchon's affinities with Fariña's sensibilities and work are recorded on the dust jacket of Fariña's 1966 novel, *Been Down So Long It Looks Like Up To Me,* where he writes, "[t]his book comes on like the Hallelujah Chorus done by 200 kazoo players with perfect pitch. . . . In spinning his yarn [Fariña] spins the reader as well, dizzily into a microcosm that manges to be hilarious, chilling, sexy, profound, maniacal, beautiful and outrageous all at the same time."[7] Pynchon's own fiction shows some resemblance to what he perceives to be the paradoxical rhetorical effects of Fariña's work and its ability to "spin the reader" (combining euphoria and chaos) into a world which is hyperbolic and fantastic and yet, composed as it is of contemporary materials, familiar.

In 1960, after graduation from Cornell and a short respite in Greenwich Village, Pynchon went to work as a technical writer for Boeing Aircraft in Seattle. During his two years at Boeing, Pynchon worked on a number of guided missile projects and wrote an article for *Aerospace Safety* entitled "Togetherness" which described safety techniques for the airlifting of IM-99A missiles. Certainly his experience as an engineering physics major at Cornell and a technical writer at Boeing gave Pynchon the background necessary to incorporate as metaphors the numerous scientific concepts which pervade his work. The title of "Togetherness," however, suggests the ironic attitude that Pynchon must have taken towards his work at Boeing, as is suggested in these headlines from the article: "One mistake and a lot of money has been wasted when you're moving a missile to its new home. It's a job requiring detailed safety on all sides. Togetherness, then, is the word."[8] The merging in these phrases of nostalgic domesticity with the sinister reality of what missiles are for (disguised by the homeliness of the language) prefigures the typically parodic intonations of Pynchon's fiction, where "reality" is packaged in metaphors that reveal the fantasies and romanticized desires of a culture bound over to deathly designs beneath the camouflage of utility, community ("togetherness"), and domesticity (the missiles' "new home").

While at Boeing, Pynchon continued writing fiction, publishing "Low Lands" and the widely anthologized "Entropy" in 1960, and "Under the Rose" in 1961. He most certainly must have been working on *V.* during those years. He completed *V.* in Mexico after he left Boeing, and with its publication in 1963 Pynchon's career as novelist begins, along with his virtual disappearance from the public scene. We might speculate endlessly on the reasons for this disappearance – shyness, xenophobia, paranoia, a mania for privacy, or, as David Seed suggests, a desire to imitate poets from the goliards to the Beats by becoming a nomad, "a writer at large."[9] But whatever personal motives lie behind his reclusiveness, Pynchon has been satisfied to let his writing stand as the signature and representation of his public life.

Accorded the Faulkner Foundation Award for his first novel, loudly acclaimed at the age of twenty-six as a major new figure in contemporary letters, Pynchon apparently receded into unknown regions – possibly rural Northern California, the anonymity of Southern California, or self-exile in Mexico. In 1964, his story "The Secret Integration" was published, and two sections from *The Crying of Lot 49* came out in popular magazines – *Esquire* and *Cavalier* – before that novel was published in 1966. David Seed has suggested that at least three versions of *The Crying of Lot 49* exist: an early manuscript (accepted for publication by J. P. Lippincott) from which the two excerpts in *Cavalier* and *Esquire* came; a review copy version, which reflected minor revisions from the original manuscript; and the published version, which reflects more (mostly minor) revisions. Seed states that a comparison of these versions "sheds a fascinating light on Pynchon's compositional methods and on his scrupulous care over the smallest details of phrasing."[10] The various editions of the novel since its original publication continue to reflect this scrupulosity in the many minor changes between editions.

The Crying of Lot 49 won the Richard and Hilda Rosenthal Foundation Award of the National Institute of Arts and Letters, although critical acclaim for the novel, as we shall see below, was less enthusiastic than it was for *V.* In 1966 Pynchon also published his most important piece of nonfiction, "A Journey into the Mind of Watts," an evocative description of the black ghetto in Los Angeles, then torn by race riots and, in Pynchon's words, "impacted in the heart of this [Los Angeles'] white fantasy . . . a pocket of bitter reality."[11] *Gravity's Rainbow,* published in 1973 and widely considered to be Pynchon's major work, is an encyclopedic, epic novel that, in Scott Simmon's phrase, purveys an "historical and cultural synthesis of Western actions and fantasies."[12] Pynchon's third novel received an abundance of critical praise and won the National Book Award (shared with Isaac Bashevis Singer's *A Crown of Feathers and Other Stories,* and accepted for Pynchon by a comedian, "Professor" Irwin Corey). After the publication of *Gravity's Rainbow* Pynchon won the Howells Medal of the National Institute of Arts and Letters for his collective body of work, but he rejected the prize. *Gravity's Rainbow* was also nominated for the Pulitzer Prize by the judges of the prize committee, but the committee was subsequently overruled by the Pulitzer advisory board.

Since the publication of *Gravity's Rainbow,* Pynchon had been working on a fourth novel and his work had rarely been seen in print: occasional book blurbs for such works as Peter Matthiessen's *Far Tortuga,* Tom Robbins' *Even Cowgirls Get the Blues,* Laurel Goldman's *Sounding the Territory,* and Steve Erickson's *Days Between Stations;* the "Introduction" to *Slow Learner;* a remembrance of Richard Fariña in the *Cornell Alumni News;* and a laudatory review of Gabriel García Márquez's *Love in the Time of Cholera.*[13] In 1988, at the age of 51, he won a MacArthur Foundation award, an extraordinary grant which gives recipients $1,000 times their age per year for five years, potentially renewable for life. Pynchon's fourth novel after a seventeen-year hiatus, *Vineland,* was released in December 1989. Touted as a novel that combines "elements of daytime drama and the political thriller," *Vineland* begins among the redwoods and small logging towns of northern California.[14] It portrays a group of 1960s hippies, radicals, and drug agents living in the conservative 1980s, with a plot revolving around various relationships and conspiracies embracing government agencies, spies, ex-"sting" specialists, and revolutionaries. Fellow novelist Salman Rushdie proclaimed *Vineland* a portrait of a "crazed patch of California" standing for "American itself," in which "one of America's great writers has, after long wanderings down his un-charted roads, come triumphantly home."[15] Here Pynchon con-tinues his fascination with the way in which personal lives are intertwined with political movements and actions as part of an ongoing plot only partially revealed by the narrative of "history" and contemporary life.

Coming after the relatively spectacular success of *V., The Crying of Lot 49* was greeted with mixed reviews. Sandwiched between two longer, seemingly more elaborate and complex works, it has often been regarded as Pynchon's "minor," if most accessible, novel. That first adjective is challenged by the mere presence of this collection; the second is partially confirmed (perhaps, to a large extent, because of the novel's brevity) by the novel's frequent appearance in the syllabi of college and university courses in con-temporary American fiction and by the fact that it is the most frequently translated of Pynchon's works: so far, versions of *The Crying of Lot 49* exist in Swedish, Italian, Danish, German, French (two translations), Spanish, Norwegian, Dutch, Japanese, and Polish.

Most early reviewers of *The Crying of Lot 49* insisted upon com-paring it unfavorably to the more massive *V.*. One strongly nega-tive commentator remarked upon *Crying*'s "crampedness" in rela-tion to the earlier novel, expounded upon its emerging patterns of significance becoming "progressively smaller, and refus[ing] to re-spond to the reader's (or the novelist's) efforts to inflate them other than by going limp with a modest hiss," and concluded by stating that "*Crying* is a step backwards to the art of the emblem books, a patchy collection of images propped up by claims of significance in terms which the artist hasn't proved the right to use."[16] The anonymous reviewer for *Time*, evaluating *The Crying of Lot 49* along with Leonard Cohen's *Beautiful Losers* and Fariña's *Been Down So Long It Looks Like Up To Me*, described Pynchon's novel as "a metaphysical thriller in the form of a pornographic comic strip," then lumped all three novels together as examples of "the gibberish literature that is currently being published as fast as it can be gibbered."[17] Less reductively, Roger Shattuck cited *The Crying of Lot 49* as "a short, crisp afterthought to *V.*"; Granville Hicks described *Crying* as "a tenth as long as *V.*, . . . considerably easier to follow, and . . . just as funny"; and the reviewer for *Newsweek* stated that *Crying* "seems to be an outgrowth of *V.*" – like *V.*, a quest novel, but "the seeker and the specific object of the search are quite different in 'Lot 49,' simpler, clearer – and a lot funnier."[18]

Though negative or reductive views of *The Crying of Lot 49* seemed to prevail, some reviewers found the novel more than just an "afterthought" to, or a more popular ("funnier," "simpler") version of, *V.* Richard Poirier, perhaps Pynchon's most incisive critic, wrote in the *New York Times* that in *The Crying of Lot 49* Pynchon evidences "a tenderness, largely missing from our literature since Dreiser, for the very physical waste of our yearnings, for the anonymous scrap heap of Things wherein our lives are finally joined. The Pynchon who can write with dashing metaphorical skill about the way humans have become Things, can also reveal a beautiful and heartbreaking reverence for the human penetration of the Thingness of this country, the signatures we make on the grossest evidence of our existence."[19] Yet even with this laudatory description of what he felt to be the novel's strongest aspect – its ability to capture the sheer materiality of American life in its "tryst with America" – Poirier had reservations about the role given to Oedipa Maas, arguing that "it is impossible to divorce from her limitations the large rhetoric about America at the end of the novel. This is unfortunate simply because Oedipa has not been given character enough to bear the weight of this rhetoric."[20] Perhaps the most laudatory review of the novel was that of Stephen Donadio, who reviewed *The Crying of Lot 49* along with Fariña's

Been Down So Long, William H. Gass's *Omensetter's Luck,* and Walker Percy's *The Last Gentleman.* Donadio wrote that *Crying* is "a desperately funny book, conceived and executed with an awesome virtuosity. The novel's tone and pace are characterized by their absolute intensity, and Mr. Pynchon's essential technique is suggested most simply by his descriptions, which invariably cut from one layer of culture to another."[21] Donadio perceptively noted in his review what has become a critical commonplace about Pynchon's fiction in general, that Pynchon's "primary observation" in *Crying* "remains central, and it is one which our current foreign policy only seems to confirm: that paranoia is the last sense of community left us."[22] Finally, Robert Sklar, in a review–essay that stands as one of the first significant critical discussions of Pynchon's fiction, argued that *The Crying of Lot 49* offers an advance over *V.* because, while the former is an exemplar of the school of black humor, the latter breaks free of categorization and succeeds in "making new and contemporary a traditional concern of the great American novelists – the creation, through the style and form of their fiction, of an imaginative system more true to their national and social system."[23] Sklar's assessment of the novel's ending, in which Oedipa awaits the "cry" of revelation that will spell her fate, foreshadows what will emerge as a major theme in Pynchon's acknowledged masterpiece, *Gravity's Rainbow,* where "that imminence of a revelation that is not yet produced is, perhaps, the aesthetic reality," and, indeed, the "reality" that most accurately pertains to contemporary millennial existence.[24]

The criticism that has emerged in the twenty-three years since the publication of *The Crying of Lot 49* suggests that it is a much more subtle and complex novel than most of its earlier reviewers, both positive and negative, allowed. Criticism of *Crying* has also made the case that this is not a minor variation on the themes and attitudes of *V.,* nor merely a "key" to *Gravity's Rainbow.* Serious and detailed analysis of the novel has revealed not only that it stands on its own, but that it contains movements and strategies latent in Pynchon's other novels. The problematic character of Oedipa Mass is a case in point. She may be seen, as Poirier has argued, as two-dimensional and thus unable to bear the weight of the novel's "sociological" rhetoric, but she may also be viewed as a most unusual "type" – a female quester searching for truth, community, significance in the interconnected realms of the phallocratic military-industrial complex and the narcissistic leisure world of southern California.[25] Cathy Davidson has argued that Oedipa is engaged in "exploring the riddle of her own identity," and though this riddle may be unsolved by the novel's end, in probing the entanglements of history, myth, contemporary lifestyles and preterite secrecies which make up the novel's substance, she effectively "challenges the cherished myths of a male-dominated society, assumptions which, in their way, comprise a Sphinx as implacable as the female figure encountered by her mythic namesake."[26] In somewhat different terms, Edward Mendelson has asserted Oedipa's importance as a quintessentially modern figure caught between the sacred and the profane. Her choice, as she walks "the hieroglyphic streets" in a world arranged "like the matrices of a great digital computer, the ones and zeroes twinned above" is "the choice between the *zero* of secular triviality and chaos, and the one which is the *ganz andere* of the sacred."[27] Even critics such as Thomas Schaub who, less optimistically than Davidson or Mendelson, regards the novel as "a tragic account of the difficulty of human action in a world whose meanings are always *either* our own *or* just beyond our reach," argues for Oedipa's importance as the central, ambiguous figure of this tragic state as she occupies a "linguistic space" between "outside and inside, between a reductive literalism in which words are mere tools standing for things, and a speculative symbolism in which words are signs capable of pointing toward realities which transcend those signs."[28] Hence, since the novel's publication, the complexity of Oedipa's stature as revolutionary, or tragic, or existential figure has been established, and like her namesake she can be seen to embody the condition of indeterminacy – which enables the act of inquiry and the scrutiny of existing conditions – that can be set against the assumptions and certainties of Western positivism.

The best early criticism of *The Crying of Lot 49*, written in the aftermath of the 1960s, stressed what might be termed the "identity crisis" that is also noted by those who have argued for the complexity of Oedipa's character: here the emphasis falls upon Oedipa's evolving role as a reader of signs and texts.[29] Oedipa must sort through a plethora of information in the attempt to arrive at the truth, or center of a conspiracy – the underground Tristero System of communication and exchange – which she seems to detect in her role as the co-executor of the enormous Pierce Inverarity estate. The system (if there is one) can be viewed as either Inverarity's legacy or its inverse: a vast series of conspiracies, historical accidents, and analogues that potentially connects (for example) a medieval postal service with the literary productions of an obscure Renaissance playwright and a series of modern-day preterite organizations, from the fanatical right-wing Peter Pinquid Society to the lovelorn Inamorati Anonymous. In observing the signs of the Tristero's presence (which may be illusory, since the signs she sees offer the possibility of being mere ciphers), and in finding her "place" within this system, Oedipa embarks upon a journey through the secular and underground worlds of contemporary southern California – a journey that compels her to inquire into the anteriority of events and their aftermath. Noting that "Pierce Inverarity" may be a play on "Dr. Moriarty," thus casting Oedipa in the role of Holmes, Joseph Slade, in the first book-length study of Pynchon, suggests that Oedipa's (arguably frustrated) quest, because it revolves around the formation of her identity as reader–detective in an indeterminate world of proliferating meanings, becomes "an endless fluctuation of sensibilities, rather like a film sprocketing through a projector. At any given moment the focus or frame changes. The self is not so much thought as lived; its existence is predicated on shifting multiple states of consciousness."[30] This conception of identity in flux is one that, earlier, Tony Tanner had noted as a general condition of contemporary American fiction, where the quest for a free, liberated self is matched by an anxiety that the "fluid" or dissipated self – without the certain strictures of law or syntax – might altogether disappear.[31] For Tanner, in a second reading of *The Crying of Lot 49* which appeared as part of his 1982 monograph on Pynchon, the question of identity in the novel comes to rest in the realm of the "excluded middle" – "a middle term for something real but unascertainable."[32] Suspended between polarities – narcissism and paranoia, totalitarian order and chaos, absolute certainty and radical uncertainty – Oedipa locates "herself" as one who mediates, "sorts," or negotiates these extremes.[33] The struggle between fluidity and form in the construction of the self has been one Richard Poirier, in several books including *A World Elsewhere* and *The Performing Self*, has located within the specific historical progressions of classic American and modern literature. Pynchon, according to Poirier, is part of this tradition or progression, a descendent of Hawthorne, Emerson, and Melville in his projection of a vision of "cultural inundation, of being swamped, swept up, counted in before you could count yourself out, pursued by every bookish aspect of life even as you try to get lost in a wilderness, in a randomness where you might hope to find your true self."[34] For Poirier, as for Tanner and Slade, Oedipa is a representative American caught in the dialectic of form and formlessness, culture and nature, legibility and the inarticulate, as she struggles to acquire the knowledge that will give some shape to her understanding of the world, and of her being in the world.

As critical interpretation of *The Crying of Lot 49* has developed, the focus has shifted somewhat from the question of the readerly identity in the novel – though this has remained constant as different ideas of identity have evolved in contemporary literary theory and philosophy – to a view of the novel as a form of communication, or as embodying certain problems and issues surrounding speech acts and the processing of information. Oedipa's role as a sorter of the information she receives, the importance of postal systems, which can either facilitate or repress the exchange of information, and the presence of such pseudoscientific esoterica as Maxwell's Demon have led readers to information theory and thermodynamics in the attempt to explain how communication works in *The Crying of Lot 49*. Anne Mangel's early article on "entropy" in the novel remains one of the most lucid discussions of how energy and information are connected in Pynchon's world, or more precisely, how the projected "heat death" of the universe can be contrasted to increasingly elaborate and sophisticated ways of gathering and dispersing information in an open, noisy system of exchange – for Mangel, the sign of "life" in Pynchon's novel.[35] Thus, especially in the *Walpurgisnacht* sequence of the novel, where Oedipa walks through an hallucinatory San Francisco nighttown, gathering more seemingly random and meaningless

11

information about the Tristero conspiracy, she comes into contact with an impressive array of underground communities and isolates; in this sense, "information" leads to "community," though it can also lead, as in *Gravity's Rainbow,* to the horror of bureaucracy when it becomes officially channelled and exfoliated. Here, in Mangel's formulation, the epistemological ambivalences of Pynchon's attitude toward information are revealed.[36] In her underground journey, Oedipa establishes connections and discovers relationships previously invisible to the naked, neutral eye, yet the rhetoric of these passages suggests that the causes and consequences of her hermeneutic activities are ambiguous – perhaps indicative of her ability to pierce through the layers of information to the hidden life of the city, or perhaps indicative of the absence of any order or truth behind the proliferation of signs and messages that make up modern existence:

> The city was hers, as, made up and sleeked so with the customary words and images (cosmopolitan, culture, cable cars) it had not been before: she had safe passage to its far blood's branchings, be they capillaries too small for more than peering into, or vessels mashed together in shameless municipal hickeys, out on the skin for all but tourists to see. . . . She touched the edge of its voluptuous field, knowing it would be lovely beyond dreams simply to submit to it; that not gravity's pull, laws of ballistics, feral ravening promised more delight. She tested it, shivering: I am meant to remember. Each clue that comes is *supposed* to have its own clarity, its fine chances for permanence. But then she wondered if the gemlike "clues" were only some kind of compensation. To make up for her having lost the direct, epileptic Word, the cry that might abolish the night. (pp. 117–18)

Hence Oedipa, like Oedipus, is placed in the tragic circumstances of not knowing whether the information she receives will lead to the reordering of existence ("the abolition of the night") or to a deeper recognition of what has been lost: one's personal past as well as the archaic, cultural past which can only be partially recovered in the activities of the dreamer or the paranoid.

Much of the critical commentary about *The Crying of Lot 49* has focused upon this conflation of epistemology, thermodynamics, and information theory as it has asked: what does all this add up to? For the novel is filled with information, codes, messages, secret languages, historical and literary allusions, puns, parodies, figures of all sorts – and yet, though these elements seduce the reader (as they seduce Oedipa) into expecting that the "cry" of revelation is at hand and that the world is filled with multiple significances, we are left with the possibility that all these "clues" will reveal only the presence of our own desire to impose meaning on a meaningless universe.[37] As Frank Kermode has suggested, the novel "is crammed with disappointed promises of significance, with ambiguous invitations to paradigmatic construction, and this is precisely Oedipa's problem. Is there a structure *au fond,* or only deceptive galaxies of signifiers?"[38] Does the novel, in the end, portray "the failure of our cultural assumptions, our philosophies, and even our imaginative constructs, to transform our lives"?[39] In terms of the second law of thermodynamics and its revision in information theory, which version of "physical reality" shall we endorse: the one which suggests that the universe is gradually running down, moving toward dissolution and chaos, and that the signs of this deevolution are everywhere, or the one which suggests that these signs signify not so much the "heat death" of entropy as the transformational flux of new life forms, new connections and new orders in the making, "a radically new conception of the nature of human identity and societal organization"?[40] Has Pynchon finally written a tragic novel, a novel of revelation, or a travesty of desire and signification in contemporary America?

Criticism of *The Crying of Lot 49* will continue to ask and answer versions of these questions, though perhaps the point is that the novel is put in the form of a question: it is, conceivably, a quest without end, an inquiry into and dramatization of our incessant desire for meaning, our will to generate signs and significance wherever we plant our feet. Framing this desire *as* a question is one of the hallmarks of postmodernist literature, to which Pynchon's work is a considerable contribution. But this formulation also leads to one of the primary questions about postmodernist fiction itself: are its speculative nature, its parodic playfulness and bookishness merely forms of diversion which lead us away from an engagement with "reality"? Molly Hite's reflection that the "excluded middle" of *The Crying of Lot 49* can be viewed as the "human world, based on the shared hopes and fears that are the tenuous connections of community . . . rendered contingent and precarious by the awesome fear of mortality" is one response to this question, but there may be a problem with the question itself: either postmodern playfulness or political engagement; either re-ified significance or meaninglessness; either paranoid community or the alienation of the individual.[41] Something, Pynchon's critics have suggested in manifold ways, must lie between the "either" and the "or" of these conditions. In coming to grips with Pynchon's novel, we are compelled to redefine the terms of such issues and, as much recent criticism of Pynchon has done, to revise our notions of uncertainty, of action and the ethical, of historical process, of the nature and construction of identity, of interpreta-tion and the work of metaphor.[42] Perhaps this is the most crucial effect of this "slim" novel: to force us into redefining our categories of thinking, or more pointedly, to force us to stop thinking cate-gorically at all.

The five essays in this volume comprise new views of *The Crying of Lot 49* in relation to this critical history. In "Borges and Pynchon: The Tenuous Symmetries of Art," Debra A. Castillo provides a "de-constructive" view of *The Crying of Lot 49*, showing how Pynchon's redaction of Jorge Luis Borges's dicta for the literary game (sym-metry, arbitrary rules, tedium) affect the nature and processes of signification in the novel. Focusing on the work of metaphor in elucidating these processes, Castillo suggests how Pynchon is aligned with literary postmodernism in both its potentialities and its limitations. John Johnston's "Toward the Schizo-Text: Paranoia as Semiotic Regime in *The Crying of Lot 49*" offers a view of the novel's processes of interpretation as they are constrained by the "regime of signs" that foster's Oedipa's paranoia in the novel. Johnston shows how interpretation becomes a political activity in Pynchon's novel, and how *The Crying of Lot 49* stands as paranoid text in relation to *Gravity's Rainbow*, which offers alternative sign-systems and, hence, alternatives to political power and paranoia.

In his essay on narrative transmission in *The Crying of Lot 49*, Bernard Duyfhuizen questions how Pynchon's novel (and Ameri-can society) transmits a cultural heritage, how that "story" can be disrupted, and in what ways its content is formed by the mechanisms of transmission themselves. Duyfhuizen's focus on cultural formations in Pynchon's novel allows him to discuss the issues of origin, power, and authority which arise out of Oedipa's becoming an executor of the Pierce Inverarity estate – an estate with the symbolic potential to stand for "all of America." In discerning the cultural deformations and "bad transmissions" of the novel, Duyfhuizen remarks upon the breakdown in communication of the culturally authorized stories which consign us to predetermined roles and functions, and our anxiety as readers when, released from these "stories," we confront a realm of interpretive freedom that is also a silent void, a blank space. In "'A Metaphor of God Knew How Many Parts': The Engine that Drives *The Crying of Lot 49*," Katherine Hayles discusses the specific poetic and narrative device of metaphor and its use in *The Crying of Lot 49* to "construct a world" in which ambivalence or ambiguity is the primary ingredient. Hayles discusses the metaphors of the novel (including the "meta-metaphor" of the quest) and argues that their ability to conjoin the concrete and the abstract allows for an "escape hatch" out of the "either/or" world that Oedipa initially inhabits. In Hayles's view the engine that drives *The Crying of Lot 49* (a novel that, crucially, employs physical principles of communication and entropy) is Pynchon's use of metaphor's expansive capability to project us beyond purely physical circumstances in (to use the novel's words) "a thrust at truth and a lie" – a paradoxically verbal projection that reflects the desire to go beyond language and to deny death, even as transcending facticity implies death.

Finally, in "A Re-cognition of Her Errand into the Wilderness," Pierre-Yves Petillon offers an evocative, wide-ranging assessment of *The Crying of Lot 49* within the interactive contexts of Pynchon's fiction, the 1950s and 1960s in America, American Puritanism, historical revolution, and eschatology. Writing from a European perspective, Petillon effectively shows how Pynchon's fiction is a layering of texts and contexts, or a kind of cultural palimpsest that reveals American attitudes towards time, expectancy, and the wilderness. This view from across the water provides a fitting conclusion to the considerations of Pynchon's "small" novel gathered here. Together, these essays are intended to provide the reader with an array of approaches – historical, linguistic, hermeneutic, narratological – with which to approach the enigmas of Pynchon's most concentrated text. As each essay acknowledges in some fashion, a critical approach to *The Crying of Lot 49* is helpful up to a point: beyond that, the reader, like Oedipa, is on her own, stranded amidst the entanglements and wonders of Pynchon's words and signs.

NOTES

1. Corbett Steinberg, in *TV Facts* (New York: Facts on File Publications, 1985), provides ratings for top-rated television programs; "Bonanza" was the highest-rated program of 1966. Raymond Olderman notes the appearance of "Wake Up America" in the May 1966 issue of *Esquire* in his *Beyond the Wasteland: A Study of the American Novel in the 1960s* (New Haven: Yale University Press, 1972), p. 120.

2. Novelist John Calvin Batchelor's somewhat whimsical "Thomas Pynchon is Not Thomas Pynchon; or, This is the End of the Plot Which Has No Name," *Soho Weekly News* (22–28 April 1976): 15–17, 21–35, claims that J. D. Salinger *is* Thomas Pynchon.

3. Peggy Kamuf, *Signature Pieces: On the Institution of Authorship* (Ithaca: Cornell University Press, 1988), p. 117.

4. Most of the details of Pynchon's biography recited here are provided by Matthew Winston, who has done more than any other critic to assemble the few available facts about Pynchon's life; see "The Quest for Pynchon," *Twentieth Century Literature* 21 (1975): 278–87. Additional "information" (or speculation concerning the lack of information) about Pynchon's life and identity is provided by the following: Thomas LeClair, "Missing Writers," *Horizon* (October 1981): 48–52; Helen Dudar, "Pynchon: The Man Who Won't Come to Dinner," *Los Angeles Times* (22 April 1974), calendar section: 6; Jules Siegel, "Who is Thomas Pynchon . . . and Why Did He Take Off with My Wife?", *Playboy* (March 1977): 97, 122, 168–70, 172, 174; Brian McHale, "Thomas Pynchon: A Portrait of the Artist as a Missing Person," *Cencrastus* 5 (1981): 2–3; Michael Hartnett, "Thomas Pynchon's Long Island Years," *Confrontation* 30/31 (1985): 44–8; and Charles Hollander, "Pynchon's Inferno," *Cornell Alumni News* 81, no. 4 (November 1978): 24–30.

5. All of Pynchon's early stories, with the exception of those that were

later integrated into his novels and "Mortality and Mercury in Vienna," are reprinted in *Slow Learner: Early Stories* (Boston: Little, Brown, 1984).

6. Richard Fariña, *Long Time Coming and a Long Time Gone* (New York: Random House, 1969): 141; 143–4.
7. Cited in Clifford Mead, *Thomas Pynchon: A Bibliography of Primary and Secondary Materials* (Elmwood Park, Ill.: Dalkey Archive Press, 1989), p. 41. Pynchon went on to write a longer introduction to the paperback reissue of *Been Down So Long* in 1983. Pynchon's reference to kazoo players in the jacket blurb suggests that the "Kazoo Choruses" of *The Crying of Lot 49* and *Gravity's Rainbow* may be minor but raucous tributes to the work of his college friend.
8. Thomas Pynchon, "Togetherness," *Aerospace Safety* 16, no. 12 (December 1960): 7.
9. David Seed, *The Fictional Labyrinths of Thomas Pynchon* (Iowa City: University of Iowa Press, 1988), p. 9.
10. David Seed, "Pynchon's Textual Revisions of *The Crying of Lot 49,*" *Pynchon Notes* 12 (1983): 39.
11. Thomas Pynchon, "A Journey into the Mind of Watts," *New York Times Magazine* (12 June 1966): 78.
12. Scott Simmon, "*Gravity's Rainbow* Described," *Critique* 16, no. 2 (1974): 55.
13. Bibliographical details regarding these scattered publications can be found in Mead, *Bibliography*, 27, 46–9.
14. Cited on the book jacket of *Vineland* (New York: Little, Brown, 1990).
15. Salman Rushdie, "Still Crazy After All These Years," *New York Times Book Review*, (14 January 1990): 37.
16. Remington Rose, "At Home with Oedipa Maas," *The New Republic* (14 May 1966): 39–40.
17. "Nosepicking Contests," *Time* (6 May 1966): 110.
18. Roger Shattuck, "Fiction a la mode" [sic], *New York Review of Books* (23 June 1966): 24; Granville Hicks, "A Plot Against the Post Office," *Saturday Review* (30 April 1966): 27; *Newsweek* (2 May 1966): 104.
19. Richard Poirier, review of *The Crying of Lot 49*, *New York Times Book Review* (1 May 1966): 43.
20. Ibid., p. 42.
21. Stephen Donadio, "America, America," *Partisan Review* 33 (1966): 449.
22. Ibid., p. 450.
23. Robert Sklar, "An Anarchist Miracle: The Novels of Thomas Pynchon," in *Pynchon: A Collection of Critical Essays*, ed. Edward Men-

delson (Englewood Cliffs, N.J.: Prentice-Hall, 1978): 95; originally published as "The New Novel, USA: Thomas Pynchon," *The Nation* (25 September 1967): 277–80.

24. Ibid., p. 96.

25. For discussions of Oedipa as quest figure, see David Cowart, *Thomas Pynchon: The Art of Allusion* (Carbondale, Ill.: Southern Illinois University Press, 1980), pp. 111–33, and Marion Brugière, "Quest Avatars in Thomas Pynchon's *The Crying of Lot 49*," *Pynchon Notes* 9 (1982): 5–16.

26. Cathy N. Davidson, "Oedipa as Androgyne in Thomas Pynchon's *The Crying of Lot 49*," *Contemporary Literature* 13 (1977): 50.

27. Edward Mendelson, "The Sacred, the Profane, and *The Crying of Lot 49*," in *Pynchon: A Collection of Critical Essays*, ed. Edward Mendelson (Englewood Cliffs, N.J.: Prentice-Hall, 1978): pp. 181, 131.

28. Thomas Schaub, *Pynchon: The Voice of Ambiguity* (Urbana: University of Illinois Press, 1981), pp. 31, 38.

29. In addition to the work on identity in the novel I summarize here, see also Manfred Pütz, *The Story of Identity: American Fiction of the Sixties* (Stuttgart: Metzlersche Verlagsbuchhandlung, 1979), pp. 130–57, and Bruce Bassoff, "In Search of Narcissus: *The Crying of Lot 49*," in his *The Secret Sharers: Studies in Contemporary Fiction* (New York: AMS Press, 1983), pp. 49–64.

30. Joseph Slade, *Thomas Pynchon* (New York: Warner Books, 1974), p. 152. Clearly, Oedipa's names bear many significances, and the discussion of these has proliferated across the range of criticism of the novel. Her names, perhaps intentionally, are a continual source of ambiguity and interpretive conflict: witness the difference between Cathy Davidson's interpretation of Oedipa's last name, "Maas," as signifying "net" or "web" in Afrikaans (43) – suggesting either her ability to connect disparate pieces of information or her entrapment in conspiracy – and Robert M. Davis's contention (in "Parody, Paranoia, and the Dead End of Language in *The Crying of Lot 49*," *Genre* 5 [1977]: 367–77) that "Maas" means "loophole" in Dutch (p. 373), thus connoting her loss of signifying power and activity.

31. See Tony Tanner, *City of Words: American Fiction 1950–1970* (New York: Harper & Row, 1971), pp. 153–73, for the application of this concept to Pynchon.

32. Tony Tanner, *Thomas Pynchon* (New York: Methuen, 1982), p. 72.

33. This is also, essentially, Schaub's argument about the novel, though he emphasizes that this condition of "being in the middle" is tragic because it makes human action nearly impossible. Alan Wilde, in

Middle Grounds: Studies in Contemporary American Fiction (Philadelphia: University of Pennsylvania Press, 1987), pp. 75–103, suggests that this is the characteristic state for a number of contemporary writers, including Pynchon, and that it offers the possibility for interpretive freedom as well as for motivational paralysis.

34. Richard Poirier, "The Importance of Thomas Pynchon," in *Mindful Pleasures: Essays on Thomas Pynchon,* ed. George Levine and David Leverenz (Boston: Little, Brown & Co., 1976), p. 29.

35. Anne Mangel, "Maxwell's Demon, Entropy, Information: *The Crying of Lot 49," TriQuarterly* 20 (1971): 194–208.

36. For a discussion of how this "informational paradox" operates in Pynchon's fiction, especially in *Gravity's Rainbow,* see my " 'A Book of Traces: *Gravity's Rainbow,"* in *Passionate Doubts: Designs of Interpretation in Contemporary American Fiction* (Iowa City: University of Iowa Press, 1986), pp. 73–94.

37. For the most complete discussion of these elements of the novel, see Cowart, *Thomas Pynchon.*

38. Frank Kermode, "The Use of the Codes," in his *The Art of Telling: Essays on Fiction* (Cambridge: Harvard University Press, 1984), p. 83. This essay was originally published in *Approaches to Poetics,* ed. Seymour Chatman (New York: Columbia University Press, 1973), pp. 68–74.

39. Roger Henkle, "Pynchon's Tapestries on a Western Wall," *Modern Fiction Studies* 17 (1971): 220.

40. Robert Nadeau, *Readings from the New Book of Nature* (Amherst: University of Massachusetts Press, 1981); p. 185.

41. Molly Hite, *Ideas of Order in the Novels of Thomas Pynchon* (Columbus: Ohio State University Press, 1983), p. 89. C. E. Nicholson and R. W. Stevenson propose a different response to the question of the novel's engagement with historical reality in " 'Words You Never Wanted to Hear': Fiction, History and Narratology in *The Crying of Lot 49," Pynchon Notes* 16 (1985): 89–109, arguing that the novel's network of "real world" references "compel the reader's attention onto a problematic historical reality from which fiction is never allowed to be a complete refuge" (106), just as Oedipa is not allowed to "escape" either into self-reflexive narcissism or into the externalized rigidity of paranoia.

42. For a discussion of *The Crying of Lot 49* as it reflects the idea of indeterminacy as affected by modern physics, see Lance Olsen, *The Ellipse of Uncertainty: An Introduction to Postmodern Fantasy* (New York: Greenwood Press, 1987), pp. 69–83. Alec McHoul, "Telegrammatology Part

I: *Lot 49* and the Post-ethical," *Pynchon Notes* 18–19 (1986): 39–54, explores the novel's "radical hermeneutics" in its deconstruction of origins and thus of traditional modes of signification and interpretation; these ideas are elaborated in McHoul's and David Wills's *Writing Pynchon: Strategies in Fictional Analysis* (Urbana: University of Illinois Press, 1989). In "Jameson's Rhetoric of Otherness and the National Allegory," *Social Text* 7 (1987): 3–35, Aijaz Ahmad discusses the relation of the political and historical unconscious to Pynchon's work at large. Bruce Herzberg, "Breakfast, Death, Feedback: Thomas Pynchon and the Technologies of Interpretation," *Bucknell Review* 27 (1983): 83–95; David Porush, *The Soft Machine: Cybernetic Fiction* (New York: Methuen, 1984), pp. 112–35; and Allon White, "Bakhtin, Sociolinguistics and Deconstruction," in *The Theory of Reading*, ed. Frank Gloversmith (New York: Barnes & Noble, 1984), pp. 123–46, argue for new senses of the act of interpretation in Pynchon's fiction. Frank Palmeri, "Neither Literally nor as Metaphor: Pynchon's *The Crying of Lot 49* and the Structure of Scientific Revolutions," *ELH* 54 (1987): 979–99, discusses revisionary views of metaphor as the vehicle of significance within the context of Thomas Kuhn's paradigm theories. Robert D. Newman, "The Quest for Metaphor in *The Crying of Lot 49*" in his *Understanding Thomas Pynchon* (Columbia: University of South Carolina Press, 1986), pp. 67–88, declares that "[i]n learning to translate the hieroglyphs [the signs of Tristero that she sees everywhere], Oedipa discovers metaphor as a means of making sense . . . an act of imaginative creation, one that asserts similarity or connection based upon the recognition of some pattern" (82). Finally, Georgianna M. Colville, *Beyond and Beneath the Mantle* (Amsterdam: Rodolpi, 1989), the first book-length study of *The Crying of Lot 49*, offers a feminist reading of Pynchon's novel.

2

Borges and Pynchon: The Tenuous Symmetries of Art

DEBRA A. CASTILLO

Nostros (la indivisa divinidad que opera en nostros) hemos soñado el mundo. Lo hemos soñado resistente, misterioso, ubicuo en el espacio y firme en el tiempo; pero hemos consentido en su arquitectura tenues y eternos intersticios de sinrazón para saber que es falso.
—Jorge Luis Borges[1]

You can put together clues, develop a thesis, or several, about why characters reacted to the Tristero the way they did, why the assassins came on, why the black costumes. You could waste your life that way and never touch the truth.
—Driblette, *The Crying of Lot 49*

IN 1967 John Barth published an article inspired by his love for the Argentinean poet and short story writer Jorge Luis Borges entitled "The Literature of Exhaustion," in which he set the Argentinean master into a more general context that included Joyce, Beckett, and Kafka. It is not necessary to review the history of the readings, rereadings, and misreadings of Barth's article, an appreciative reception that turned the "literature of exhaustion" into a critical commonplace. I would like, however, to note two rather interesting consequences of Barth's essay. First, while Borges was well known and much appreciated in Latin America both in his own right and as a precursor of the "Boom" writers of the 1960s, for many inhabitants of North America Barth's article revealed a startling new talent on the world literary scene. Borges was, through Barth, reinvented as an American author, becoming for Barth's readers, if not for Barth himself, the "contemporary" of U.S. fiction writers like John Hawkes, William Gass, Donald Barthelme, Thomas Pynchon, and Barth himself. Indeed, in a later reflection on his famous article entitled "The Literature of Re-

21

plenishment,"[2] Barth becomes, unconsciously perhaps, seduced by this now pervasive comprehension of contemporary literary history; he there categorizes Borges as a postmodernist, along with such writers as those listed above, and also includes as his contemporaries Colombian Nobel laureate Gabriel García Márquez (the quintessential Boom author) and Italo Calvino.

The second point I wish to make is that this curious violation of chronology in the conflation of two or three generations of writers is, in a bizarre way, appropriate, as it both reflects and respects the implicit aesthetics of Borges's work. Just so, Borges himself often violates temporal schemes in order to have books converse with each other across the shelves of a library; in one instance among many, Borges resurrects his precursor, Leopoldo Lugones (1874–1938), in order to have him comment on Borges' own recently released miscellany of short sketches and poetry (*El hacedor*, 1960). In a like manner a critic who carried out in practice the implications of a postmodern conflation of temporal schema might speculate on the possible influences of Thomas Pynchon's novels on the Borges short stories of the 1940s and 1950s, instead of merely producing a more conventional influence study that respects standard chronology. My aim here is more modest: I propose that in reading the two authors together we can uncover some of the more puzzling aspects of Pynchon's aesthetics.

A reader coming from Pynchon to Borges cannot help but notice the startling congruity of styles between the American and the Latin American. Both are masters of what we might call a desperate comedy of inaccessibility, marked and defined by an adamant insistence on a few intensely imaged symbols: in Borges, the dreams, labyrinths, mirrors, and tigers so familiar to his readers. Pynchon shares the dreams and the labyrinths, but for him, modern media substitutes for the Borgesian mirrors, and technological marvels are his tigers. Likewise, both authors rely heavily on a few insistently reiterated metaphors: in both, we are drawn into the temptations and unrealities of mathematics and the physical sciences; in both, as John Updike notes of Borges, "we move . . . beyond psychology, beyond the human, and confront . . . the world atomized and vacant. Perhaps not since Lucretius has a poet so definitely felt men as incidents in space."[3] Borges' tenuously imagined librarians, his dreamers within the dream, his immortals, and his metaphysical gauchos resonate comfortably with the equally tenuous characters of *The Crying of Lot 49* – Oedipa and Mucho Maas, Pierce Inverarity, Genghis Cohen, Professor Bortz, Dr. Hilarius, names so comically overdetermined that, like the Tristero itself, they are atomized and exploded by their very semantic richness.

Such relativization and negation reaches into all levels of these confections. Carefully constructed and firmly established plot lines are demolished at a stroke, infected by impossibly corrupt or undeniably fictitious elements; even at the micro-level of a noun clause the author gives us nothing firm and resistant without also suggesting the irrational fault lines of the fiction's architecture, linking abstract nouns to concrete modifiers and the reverse. From Borges: "innumerable contrición" ("innumerable contrition"), "rigorosamente extraño" ("rigorously strange"), "el interminable olor" ("the interminable fragrance"), "ese pasado equiívoco y lánguido" ("that equivocal and languid past"), "la casi infinita muralla china" ("the almost infinite Chinese wall"), "se recluyó en un palacio figurativo" ("he retired to a figurative place"), and "neustro destino . . . es espantoso porque es irreversible y de hierro" ("our destiny is horrifying because it is irreversible and of iron").[4] Similarly, chosen almost at random from *The Crying of Lot 49*: "the unimaginable Pacific," which "stayed inviolate and integrated or assumed the ugliness at any edge into some more general truth" (55), or Manny Di Presso's warning, "Not so loud . . . They're watching. With binoculars" (57), or the characters' anticipation of a "solid silence, air somehow waiting for them" (59). The children in Pynchon who sort reality from dream (117–18) recall Borges' dreamer who dreams a real man in "The Circular Ruins"; the unlikely addendum on the Tristero stamp pasted into Cohen's copy of the stamp catalogue reminds the reader of the singularly corrupt copy of Borges' 1917 edition of *The Anglo-American Cyclopaedia* which testifies to the existence of Tlön in "Tlön, Uqbar, Orbis Tertius"; and Oedipa's hypothetical amnesiac seizures which prevent her from grasping the essential truth (95) parallel the frustrated searches of any number of Borgesian librarians who hypothesize the existence of a Book of Books in the infinite stacks of the Library of Babel, or the philosophers who attempt to discover the name of God written in the stripes of a tiger.

Certainly, both Pynchon's and Borges' dramas of dazzling combinatorics and differential decay respond to the pre-posthum(or)-ous dissection of the postmodern (in Pynchon, also post-postal) condition. We can distinguish in both the wary, weary recognition that the search for eternal verities – God, science, a center – are inevitably conditioned and contaminated by the seeking mind, that the unrealities of existence militate against the very possibility of the search, much less its successful conclusion. In the words of the physicist Stephen Hawking:

> If Euclidean space-time stretches back to infinite imaginary time, or else starts at a singularity in imaginary time, we have the same problem as in the classical theory of specifying the initial state of the universe. God may know how the universe began, but we cannot give any particular reason for thinking it began one way or another. On the other hand, the quantum theory of gravity has opened up a new possibility, in which there would be no boundary to space-time and so there would be no need to specify the behavior at the boundary. There would be no singularity at which the laws of science broke down and no edge of space-time at which one would have to appeal to God or some new law to set the boundary conditions for space-time. One could say: "The boundary condition of the universe is that it has no boundary." The universe would be completely self-contained and not affected by anything outside itself. It would neither be created or destroyed. It would just BE.[5]

The disturbing and seductive corollary for fiction is clear. No longer is the fictional universe bounded by the classical rules of verisimilitude and plausibility; instead, it is conceived, in a fictional parallel to quantum physics, as a self-contained game with the sole responsibility of maintaining consistency with its own rules. For Borges and, I will argue, for Pynchon as well, the rules are deceptively simple; in the words that Borges gives his character Herbert Quain: "Yo reivindico para esa obra . . . los rasgos esenciales de todo juego: la simetría, las leyes arbitrarias, el tedio" ("I revindicate for this work the essential elements of every game: symmetry, arbitrary rules, tedium").[6]

The first element, symmetry, suggests the structuring force and subject that stands before any access to the game; pattern and congruence are the foremost qualities of these structuring elements. From one point of view, the requirement of symmetry will intimate the formal principle of structure in a given text – the parameters of the paradigm, as it were. Symmetry is the frame of the picture, the geography of the Monopoly board, the necessary precondition for defining the nature of the artifact. It is also, simultaneously and conversely, an active principle: the will to form which imposes order on apparent chaos, the closure without boundaries of the solipsistic circle, the miracle machine that creates plot out of disorganized fragments. The end of Pynchon's novel, Georgianna M. Colville suggests, only returns us to the moment before opening the book when we were awaiting "the crying of lot 49."[7] The book has announced itself, defined itself, and, in a peculiarly postmodern variation of this tightly symmetrical construction, put quotation marks around its own title – the key to unlock this structure – thus displacing formal symmetry into an active, metafictional shadow writing.

The second Borgesian requirement, arbitrary rules, corresponds to and derives from the first. Borges' surprisingly apt recognition is that *all* rules – generally mythologized in common practice as unchanging, eternal, necessary laws handed down from God or his avatars – are in fact as entirely arbitrary as the rules governing more recognizably fictive games. Why does a player have to go to jail in Monopoly when she lands on a specific square? Are the structures for fines just and equitable? Are property prices fair? Why can we play partners in bridge and not in chess? Since structures are conceived by humans to fill a particular need, they are of necessity tentative and egocentric. It follows that they are also recognizably arbitrary, and not required to correspond to any rules outside the game. A set of rules, then, may be uniquely applicable to a particular fiction; in practice, habitual metaphors and obsessive images constrain the set of options available to an author. Within the structure of the game, the rules, though arbitrary in conception, become the norm which, once imposed, is inviolate. It does not help the player to question, within the bounds of Monopoly, for example, the "fairness" of the written set of procedures for playing Monopoly. The player has to "play by the rules" or leave the game. What does *not* follow, however, is that the rules of the game in postmodern fiction are necessarily available in toto to the players. Often the instruction sheet is missing or incomplete. In fact, in both Borges and Pynchon, one of the primary problems for the characters is to determine the set of rules that governs their particular circumstances; naturally, they can never be certain that the rules they do manage to deduce are more than the peculiar constructions of their own minds.

Finally, the game is "tedious"; for, while the players can engage in an infinite number of games, or a single eternal game, the elements of the game are finite and respond to a mathematically determinable number of combinations which, given a long enough playing time, must recur. The classical expression of this rule in Borges can be found in "The Library of Babel." The head librarian of one of the hexagons (the primary spatial unit of the library) derives a basic set of axioms to describe the operation of the library: "de esas premisas incontrovertibles dedujo que la Biblioteca es total y que sus anaqueles registran todas las posibles combinaciones de los veintitantos símbolos ortográficos (número, aunque vastísimo, no infinito) o sea todo lo que es dable expresar. . . . Si un eterno viajero la atravesara en cualquier dirección, comprobaría al cabo de los siglos que los mismos volúmenes se repiten en el mismo desorden (que, repetido, sería un orden: el Orden)". "From these incontrovertible premises he deduced that the Library is total and that its stacks contain all the possible combinations of the twenty-odd orthographic symbols (a vast, but not infinite, number), that is, it contains all that it is possible to say. . . . If an eternal traveler were to cross it in any direction, he would prove after centuries of travel that the same volumes repeat themselves in the same disorder (which, repeated, would be an order: the Order").[8]

Any game invented by humans, then, can never be more than *apparently* open-ended. In the more radical sense, all games are by definition repetitious, total, uncontaminated, and closed: in short, tedious. It could be argued, of course, that this repetition conditions and is conditioned by the nature of the game itself. The return to the moment just prior to the beginning of the text in *The Crying of Lot 49* is created by the Borgesian revindication of the fictive process: the return to the beginning of the game, so as to start playing once more; the return of that redundant, overdetermined element repressed in the opening moves so as to allow the game to continue.

In what follows, I will read *The Crying of Lot 49* as a symmetrical structure (at the level of plot), as a quest for a hidden set of rules (through the protagonist's grasp of essential metaphors), and as a Borgesian tedium. One caveat is required, however. Any categorical separation of the novel is as artificial as the object of analysis: the structure is inevitably disrupted by the tenuous and arbitrary interstices of irrationality; the apparently arbitrary responds to a higher order; the tedium is necessarily masked by the excitement of the game.

Symmetry

As Tony Tanner has argued, plotting about plot is at the very heart of *The Crying of Lot 49*: "Pynchon's work is full of plots and codes — at every level, from political plots, spies, conspiracies and all kinds of private forms of communication, to larger, national, global, even metaphysical and religious questions concerning the possible presence or absence of plots."[9] The semantic range of the key word, "plot," easily runs the range of possibilities outlined by the *American Heritage Dictionary*: ". . . a measured area of land; lot . . . A ground plan. . . . The series of events consisting of an outline of the action of a narrative or drama . . . A secret plan to accomplish a hostile or illegal purpose, a scheme." In all of his plotting, Pynchon is scrupulously fair, warning the reader from the very beginning that this "lot" is a "plot" (a circumscribed place, perhaps a gameboard) and that the plot (narrative) is always and only a plot (secret plan) which, if uncovered and displayed, will demonstrate only the machinations of the game. Hence, Rodney Driblette warns Oedipa Maas, "[i]t isn't literature, it doesn't mean anything," or later, "[y]ou can put together clues, develop a thesis, or several. . . . You could waste your life that way and never touch the truth. Wharfinger supplied words and a yarn. I gave them life. That's it." (80)

Such admonitions serve as both warning against and invitation for overreading of the novel, and indeed Pynchon's critics (we scholarly detectives) have delighted in taking Oedipa's role, searching for revelations that are, seemingly, absurdly easy to discover.[10] Thus, to take only one recent example, Colville devotes the fourteen pages of her second chapter, "From Words to Worse," to a detailed decrypting of the possible meaning systems hidden in the patently symbolic names of the novel's characters. This is all great fun, of course, an intellectual game, as Colville herself joyously and self-consciously recognizes: "Oedipa could just as well have been Oedipussy [a scandalous reference to a James Bond character], but there comes a time when the bouncing has to stop."[11] The name anchors description – in Foucault's words, "the name is the *end* of discourse"[12] – providing a superficial point of reference, an index of functionality. It is a curious feature of Pynchon's novel that the most functional of all things – the solid, stolid clues, so recalcitrant in their thingness, their quiddity, their resistance to the allegorizing impetus – tip perilously into a sort of hyperrational variation. The absolute blurs into the hypothetical, the irreducible, individualizing name into the generalized function of naming, as if the one inescapable flaw of even the most rational formula is the fundamental suspicion of a merely constructed symmetry underlying the precisions of mathematically defined calculation. There is a certain tense distancing between name and thing that recognizes and mocks efforts at detection or interpretation; a creeping inconclusiveness and dematerialization taints efforts to find definitive answers: "San Narciso was a name; an incident among our climatic records of dreams and what dreams became among our accumulated daylight" (178). Always, the name is the figure to suggest the unnamed or unnameable, as in Oedipa's first description of the city as "like so many named places," which, inversely, suggests other, unnamed places. The city and its name are contaminated by technology and abstraction: "it was less an identifiable city than a grouping of concepts," a "circuit card" of hieroglyphic streets and houses reflecting back (how can it not do so, with Narcissus as a nominal referent?) the observing eye of the automotive self (24).

Pynchon's openly allegorical names playfully generate a series of potential stories, perhaps even necessary fictions, but he gives us both too much and too little nominative significance. In hesitating between dream and materiality, the overdetermined and the literal, he provokes a ritual reluctance to choose a single story, a single identity, an unequivocal name, a clear motive, a definitive solution. It is in this respect that Pynchon's plot, while following the outward form of the detective novel or quest narrative, denies that form's most basic expectations for a final revelation (as opposed to a decision merely to arbitrarily end this particular game). This contrasts with a theory of narrative structure *as game* present in the type of text described by Roland Barthes in *S/Z*:

> Expectation thus becomes the basic condition for truth: truth, these narratives tell us, is what is *at the end of* expectation. This design brings narrative very close to the rite of initiation (a long path marked with pitfalls, obscurities, stops, suddenly comes out into the light); it implies a return to order, for expectation is a disorder: disorder is supplementary, it is what is forever added on without solving anything, without finishing anything; order is complementary, it completes, fills up, saturates, and dismisses everything that risks adding on: truth is what completes, what closes.[13]

The problem posed by both Barthes and by Pynchon's fictional hermeneut, the housewife-cum-literary-detective Oedipa Maas, is a question of reading and interpretation, of apertures and closed doors, of right turns and dead ends in a gradually uncovered pattern of revelations. The postmodern game, however, is quite other. Oedipa is seeking a plot, a pattern; obligingly, the narrative complies. She expects seduction – "Either he made up the whole thing . . . or he bribed the engineer over at the local station to run this, it's all part of a plot, an elaborate, seduction, *plot*" (31) – and is seduced. She hopes to find revelations, and so is overwhelmed by a substantial surplus of them. She is obsessed with "bringing something of herself" to Inverarity's legacy ("She would give [his business interests] order, she would create constellations" [90]), and she finds the constellations all too easy to construct, the connections so embarrassingly simple that she begins to suspect a plot behind the plot, begins to suspect herself of either paranoia or overinterpretation. The traditional detective, as Holquist notes, is able to triumph "because he alone in a world of credulous men holds to the Scholastic principle of *adequatio rei et intellectus*, the adequation of mind to things, the belief that mind, given enough time, can understand everything. There are no mysteries, there is only incorrect reasoning. This is the enabling discovery Poe makes for later authors; he is the Columbus who lays open the world of *radical rationality* which is where the detectives have lived ever since."[14] Oedipa's problem is that, curiously, her world begins to limit itself to her hypothesized equation.

For this postmodern detective, radical rationality becomes not an enabling discovery, but a crippling handicap. Oedipa's clues either point too clearly and too obviously in one direction – the Tristero, the postmodern equivalent of "the butler did it" – or proliferate in a branching labyrinth of potential directions too multiple to be followed, or circle back endlessly to the ambiguous, multiply significant "crying of lot 49." The clear, strong impetus of the formulaic novel is somehow diverted into its near opposite; rational reconstruction falters at the edge of a shimmering void, a mirage of understanding. Chaos, rather than ceding to order and reason, resists interpretation, not as an actively malevolent force, but as a kind of deadening inertia – Pynchon calls it "entropy" – barely sensed under an opaque surface. It is not so much even a matter of beginnings and endings, or posing a puzzle and promising a solution, as it is a question of muddling through and confronting an inexplicable excess in two almost mutually exclusive forms of representation, equally deadly and deadening. There is both too much evidence and too many connections between clues, yet this overabundance of "something" fades into "nothing" (the clues are real, but strangely insubstantial), leaving an uncanny trace trapped in an "excluded middle" between meaninglessness and meaning. The purposeful movement of the detective fades into Oedipa's exhausted overstimulation and her dawning awareness that even the most frenetic mental and physical exertion merely disguises an external stasis and an almost entirely *internal* perception of an advance in the plot.

This novel is in many ways more *about* its genre than *of* it, and the repeated "almost" of my last few remarks reflects recognition of an inherent stress point in even the most formulaic works, an incipient deconstruction from within. As Geoffrey Hartman recognizes, "the trouble . . . with the [mass-market] detective novel is not that it is moral but that it is moralistic; not that it is popular but that it is stylized; not that it lacks realism but that it picks up the latest realism and exploits it." Pynchon's literary detective novel puts pressure precisely upon these stress points, exploiting and emphasizing these troubling features, suggesting, paradoxically, that these meditations on genre, in departing from formula, return to a purified version of it. What is most surprising is that such a sharpening of attention seems so remarkable. Hartman continues: "A voracious formalism dooms [the detective novel] to seem unreal, however 'real' the world it describes. In fact, as in a B movie, we value less the driving plot than the moments of lyricism and grotesquerie that creep into it."[15] A "B" movie, an Ian Fleming thriller, already approach the boundary dividing genre fiction from trash on the one hand and elite art on the other. Or are both hands the same hand, a sleight of hand, as it were? Pynchon's extraordinary feeling for rubbish, well documented by Tanner, attests to his ability to sift together commonplace and existential angst in his feverish and ferociously funny depictions of billboards, TV programs, department store Muzak.[16] As Mucho says, "'It was only the sign in the lot, that's what scared me. . . . We were a member of the National Automobile Dealers' Association. N.A.D.A. Just this creaking metal sign that said nada, nada, against the blue sky. I used to wake up hollering" (144). The echoes of Hemingway's stoics and Fitzgerald's famous billboard (the eyes of T. J. Eckelburg in *The Great Gatsby*) are obvious in this throw-away spoof/homage to the urban novel of high modernism. The reader in search of a profound meaning will find exactly what Pynchon has already offered openly: nothing.

This reversal of the paradigm of the Faustian quester transformed into a jester striving to decode a vast urban text and finding only the text writ large accords with Robbe-Grillet's discussion of the French "new novel" of the 1950s as an inverted detective story: "The exhibits described in a thriller . . . provide a fairly accurate illustration of the situation. The various elements collected by the detectives . . . would all seem at first sight to call for an explanation, [but] whether they conceal or reveal a mystery, these elements that defy all systems have only one serious, objective quality – that of being there."[17] The novelist Robbe-Grillet suddenly sounds uncannily similar to physicist Stephen Hawking, who can dismiss God in favor of a self-contained universe defined by simple "being," with no religious overtones.

At issue is no longer a matter of rational understanding of the truth, but another enabling/disabling condition – that which forces us to recognize the world as it is, in the middle between an elegantly posed problem and its hermeneutically satisfying conclusion, in the world of a text whose only significance lies in its existence as text. And further we are forced to recognize the subterfuge of languages: as Jameson says of Raymond Chandler, "he feels in his language a kind of material density and resistance: even those clichés and commonplaces take on an outlandish resonance [and] are used between quotation marks, as you would delicately expose some interesting specimen."[18] The clue becomes a word, a fragile verbal arabesque delicately framed between figurative quotation marks, an unreadable – if undeniably aesthetic – cipher, a zero degree artifact of writing.

As in Borges, what is essentially at issue is another, unsought surplus: the irreducible remainder of the individual self, a peculiar variation on the self-consciously reflective narrative mirroring typical of the postmodern text. The search for the other intimates and initiates a search for the self within the overlap and reversal between the various and overdetermined stories of the corpses of soldiers and mail carriers that figuratively litter the novel and the *corpus* (the corpse of the story itself).

Oedipa seeks not only the logically satisfying rational reconstruction of a hidden (killed) story, but also that which precedes the beginning of the story, the pre-history (fully one third of *The Crying of Lot 49* consists of interpolated stories that seek to anticipate or explain some aspect of the story that Oedipa attempts to reconstruct), the pre-lude (before the game), the pre-face (can we hypothesize about the original face behind the grimaces Dr. Hilarius uses in his therapy sessions?) – all that exists at the boundary of the legitimate story. Solution of the ostensible mystery only reconfirms the existence of this impossible boundary, dooming the protagonist to yet another reenactment by anticipation of the subtext, the as-yet-unenacted, multiply ambiguous crying of lot 49.

In the end, as is the case in the Borges detective story explicated by J. Hillis Miller, "the reader feels himself or herself left with nothing in hand but the artifice of a dead figure."[19] The stamps, painstakingly described in the novel as slight, morbid variations on the more familiar stamps in circulation, identified by the experts as forgeries through a questionably reliable addendum to a standard reference catalogue, serve as a final example of the duplicitous, reduplicated text both hidden from and in clear view of later scholars, which in its various stages of corruption haunts the entire work. The stamps, like the play *The Courier's Tragedy,* the Baby Igor movie *Cashiered,* and the Nazi war tales stored in the mobile face of Dr. Hilarius, almost too easily offer themselves as what Stephen Heath has called the "scriptural of narrative," with both religious/mythic and redundantly literary overtones.[20] Pynchon and Borges show us only too clearly how little we learn from the neat, rational, hermeneutical process and what abysses of ignorance these processes uncover.

The Crying of Lot 49 configures itself as a "double" escape fiction, not only for the reader but also for the characters and the narrator, who call up a scriptural of narrative most emphatically defined as an escape from literature itself – this despite the inescapable presence of a central text of evidence and artifact evoked through Wharfinger's play and the assorted "literary" and "historical" studies that surround it. Here, there is a recognition that there is no escape, despite buffering, despite "insulation" (one of Pynchon's key words), and despite efforts to retain a certain irreducible remainder of the self free from contamination:

> What did she desire to escape from? Such a captive maiden . . . soon realizes that her tower, its height and architecture, are like her ego only incidental: that what really keeps her where she is is magic, anonymous and malignant, visited upon her from outside and for no reason at all. Having no apparatus except gut fear and female cunning to examine this formless magic, to understand how it works, how to measure its field strength, count its lines of force, she may fall back on superstition . . . (21–2)

Certain moments, Pynchon's novel suggests, are available only by a symmetrical balancing of magic and experimental physics, of myth and rational focus. They are accessible only in the mutual deconstruction of both competing belief systems. Furthermore, it is in moments like these that we catch a glimpse of an Oedipa entirely different from the typical suburban housewife who goes to Tupperware parties, gets drunk on the kirsch in the fondue, and has a fondness for popular television programs like "Bonanza." Interlinearly, we recall a buried remainder of another self – scholar adventurer or scientist – exercising vigorously those "psychic muscles that no longer existed" (161): the reader of *Scientific American*, the woman familiar with Cornell University, Jay Gould, experimental physics, and the music of Bartok (9–10). The housewife is also the hermeneutical critic with an eye for symmetry in her fourfold analysis of what McHale calls "the epistemological cul-de-sac into which she has backed herself."[21] Oedipa theorizes that either she has stumbled onto the Tristero's plot, or she has been self-deceived into believing in the Tristero, or she has been deceived by a plot against her, or she is fantasizing some such plot. The range of "solutions," then, runs the gamut from the epistemological to the psychological. Oedipa herself, insulation lost, breathless and pregnant with the cloudy ghosts of her superstitions/suppositions, "hoped she was mentally ill; that that's all it was" (171), but she cannot escape the tenuous persistence of the other alternatives, just as she cannot ignore the ghosts of the other great "as if" troubling her quest: "As if their home cemetery in some way still did exist. . . . As if the dead really do persist, even in a bottle of wine" (99), or in the exhaled smoke of a cigarette filtered through charcoal made from the bones of heroes. As if the symmetries of plot do have some transcendental meaning; as if, frighteningly, the self IS, self-contained and without boundary.

Arbitrary Rules

The second of the essential elements for the Borgesian game is that it have a finite set of arbitrarily determined but consistently applied rules. At the heart of this rule system is what Jacques Derrida in another context describes as "the law of economy . . . acknowledged in the movement from one constituted figure to another at least implicitly constituted figure, and not in the production itself of the figure."[22] This movement of metaphor, enabled by a buried resemblance between the terms, functions partly as a displacement, partly as a translation, and partly as a way of addressing an unknown, ciphered "X," figured (or disfigured) in and by the text. In *The Crying of Lot 49* Pynchon marks, unambiguously but with crafty complexity, both the instances of the rule of metaphor and its practice.

First rule: "Now here was Oedipa, faced with a metaphor of God knew how many parts; more than two anyway. With coincidences blossoming these days wherever she looked, she had nothing but a sound, a word, Tristero, to hold them together" (109). No longer can metaphor be defined as the imagination's bridge, flung between two concepts. The wild proliferation of evidence means that Oedipa has to consider higher geometries and mental bridges in more than merely the standard three dimensions. That problem, however, is minor compared to the other: even if she could imagine bridges, the grounding for metaphor would still be slipping away beneath her feet. The word, the sign, "Tristero," becomes arbitrary, "nothing but a sound." It exempts itself from the internal meaning system of the English language, then reestablishes itself as a motive for metaphor, translating, representing, or inducing by its very sound the force moving between figure and figure. And that force is impossible to understand, although Oedipa can recognize its existence readily enough.

Second rule: "The act of metaphor then was a thrust at truth and a lie, depending where you were: inside, safe, or outside, lost" (129). I pause at this image, in which the definition of metaphor enacts metaphor through a conflation of the concepts of "home" ("inside, safe") and "truth," as the chain adduced by Oedipa seems suspiciously binary: truth–inside–safe vs. lie–outside–lost. Once again, however, the force of the statement lies not in the chain adduced, but in the emphasis on the "thrust," the force that moves metaphor through the image, compromising the comfort of homeliness, the housewifely history of being, contaminating it with the distinctive force of its passage. It is the force itself – not the image but the process – that is clearly at issue in Oedipa's meditations on the act of metaphor. This "force" is to be imagined less in traditional metaphorical than in mathematical terms, as a vector, in the example that immediately follows upon Oedipa's generalization. In her conversation with the homeless man with the DTs, his alcoholism-induced trembling offers Oedipa, through "the high magic of low puns," a dazzling isomorphism with the mathematical concept of the infinitesimal, dt (derivative with respect to t), otherwise defined as the "time differential," that is, "a vanishingly small instant in which change had to be confronted at last for what it was . . . where velocity dwelled in the projectile though the projectile be frozen in midflight, where death dwelled in the cell though the cell be looked in on at its most quick" (129). The critic's job, like Oedipa's, lies in the intuitive grasp of this mental construct, the impossibly small instant in which the force of metaphorical movement can be frozen for inspection, preserving it in a still life (in Spanish, "una naturaleza muerta"). This "vanishingly small instant" is, of course, also a mental construct, a physicist's theoretical game, which, like the linguistic games of a purely theoretical version of the Tristero existing only at the level of sound, slips away and hastens decomposition even as it seems to halt momentarily the precipitous decline.

Third rule: metaphor is in itself a hallucination, an access to an unexpected place, not home, not homey, but a force slipping sideways across the merely linguistic grooves or tracks left by the passage of time: "Behind the initials was a metaphor, a delirium tremens, a trembling unfurrowing of the mind's plowshare. . . . Trembling, unfurrowed, she slipped sideways, screeching back across grooves of years" (128–9). Or later, in a much-quoted climactic recognition, Oedipa recalls

> knowing as if maps had been flashed for her on the sky, how these *tracks* ran on into others, others, knowing they laced, deepened, authenticated the great night around her. . . . For there either was some Tristero beyond the appearance of the legacy America, or there was just America and if there was just America then it seemed the only way she could continue, and manage to be at all relevant to it, was as an alien, *unfurrowed,* assumed full circle into some paranoia. (179, 182; my emphasis)

The either/or assumptions of this passage are playfully stark. Figuratively, either America will have to change for Oedipa to fit into it, its symmetrical fertile furrows going as unseeded as her brain and her womb, its amber fields of grain slipping back into a pristine, unfurrowed state of expectation, or she, the unfurrowed one in a world of burgeoning growth, must become part of the unnurturing solipsism of an alien existence. There is, one could argue, an entire philosophy of "as if" in Pynchon's short novel, a shifting map of possibilities for the unfurrowing of resemblance through the counter-factual. Clearly, as well, the metaphorical force behind the unfolding revelation – and this is the beauty and duplicity of the "as if" – makes no pretense at uncovering or duplicating the reality of the world. Instead, the work of metaphor in the novel intimates a conflicted decomposition and recomposition of language as such; in its very arbitrariness, the metaphorical language of *The Crying of Lot 49* involves a progressive dissolution and reconstitution that implicates, furthermore, the entire history of Oedipa's selfhood. This self, in turn, is metaphorized as either an unfurrowing, a slippage across the hallucinatory memory of tracks and grooves worn smooth (can Oedipa remember her own memories?), or conversely, as an unwanted furrowing, as when the cognition of the "symmetrical four" alternatives results in a figurative and inexplicable impregnation as Oedipa is seduced, finally, by her own plots. The function of the unfurrowing "as if," then, is to reestablish the tentative self as a person and as a linguistic construct from the minimal clues – perhaps entirely imaginary – of a tenuously held theory. "I am," Oedipa seems to be telling us, even if "I" persists as a metaphor for a certain kind of madness.

Fourth rule, derived from and implicit in the first three: metaphor is a desiring/desired machine. What is desired ranges from religious to purely secular revelations about the nature of the universe and the self. Pynchon, I believe, intends these concerns to be taken ironically, but also wholly seriously. The machine is, of course, a central thematic and symbolic presence in Pynchon's work, an implicit metaphorical bridge between the forces of technology and those of hallucination or dream. The point is made early in the novel with reference to Oedipa's husband, Mucho, who had suffered "exquisite torture" in his former job as a used car salesman: "He could still never accept the way each owner, each shadow, filed in only to exchange a dented, malfunctioning version of himself for another, just as futureless, automotive projection of somebody else's life. As if it were the most natural thing. To Mucho it was horrible. Endless, convoluted incest" (14). For Mucho the horror is only partly in the identification of owner and machine that makes them strictly interchangeable. Much more horrible is the futureless, unending processing of desire, the unchanging flow of people and machines, the unidentified force that limits the perceived parts of this metaphor to the traditional two poles, establishes a system of equivalences, and funnels variety into homogeneity at the exchange point of the car dealer's office.

Mucho's new job, as a disk jockey, is not much better. Instead of automobiles, he deals with tape recorders, but the system of distortion insures that, once again, a unilateral system of appropriation and exchange takes place in the working of the machine:

> Mucho thrust the mike in front of her, mumbling, "You're on, just be yourself." Then in his earnest broadcasting voice [obviously not "just being himself"], "how do you feel about this terrible thing?"
>
> "Terrible," said Oedipa.
>
> "Wonderful," said Mucho. . . . "Thank you Mrs. Edna Mosh . . . for your eyewitness account of this dramatic siege at the Hilarius Psychiatric Clinic. . . ."
>
> "Edna Mosh?" Oedipa asked.
>
> "It'll come out the right way," Mucho said. "I was allowing for the distortion on these rigs, and then when they put it on tape."
> (139)

In order to name the witness, Mucho must machinate the presentation, calculating the degree of distortion in one machine so as to compensate for it in another. He must, operating on the principle of linguistic slippage along the tracks of his tape band, find other names in order to establish his equivalences. In so doing, he misses the element in the machine that functions according to the same principles as the hidden Tristero, the appearance of work (communication, reproduction of the human voice) thrust into a slightly deviant track by severe irony: the name "Edna Mosh," mechanically reproduced in his own "earnest broadcasting voice."

To some degree, the machine that has most intrigued readers of this novel, Maxwell's box or the Nefastis Machine, is a madman's answer to these other homogenizing machines, as its function, in the hands of the adept, is to accomplish "work" – move an experimental piston – through discrimination between fast and slow molecules. I would argue, however, that the question of sorting, derived from the discussion of this machine and explicitly extended to the problems of the postal service and to Oedipa's own quest for information, functions as a colorful, highly overdetermined false lead, a kind of dream-machine. The Nefastis Machine functions most clearly as a dream *of* functioning, and works in the novel as a hallucination of utility, its meaning defined in the muted distortions of pure loss. Analogously, the role of the literary detective (Oedipa, the reader) in Pynchon's novel is less one of separating clues into valid and fraudulent than of engaging, slipwise if necessary, the system machinating what might be termed a structural incapacity to think without binary categories. To put the matter in the form of a question rather than a statement, what happens if we as readers conceive of the narrative as a progressive and strictly uninterpretable distortion rather than as jumble of zeroes and ones from which the critic, like Maxwell's Demon, sorts true from false, inside from outside, hot from cold, relevant from nonsensical? What if we were to make no claim to understand the linguistic forces and movements of *The Crying of Lot 49*, but merely to read the ion trails of their passage?

In this exemplary postmodern text, Pynchon clearly indicates to what degree any reader organizes a story by the fact of naming it and claiming for it a preferred interpretation.[23] These require an act of self-distancing that compels recognition of the arbitrary nature of the fictions we live by, and the force of language as mediating between mind and whatever we choose to consider reality. Like Borges's famous cartographer, who drew increasingly detailed maps only to discover that the topography finally described the features of his own face, Pynchon's characters, and his readers, forcibly confront how we are constituted by the unconscious projections of our particular linguistic structures, how we are dominated by the ambiguities of the "as if," and how our dreams and our language produce, rather than reflect, what we consider "truth."[24]

A variation of the figure of the cartographer recurs in Pynchon's novel through Oedipa's meditation on the painting of Remedios Varo, "Bordando el manto terrestre," which she sees in Mexico City with Pierce Inverarity. The reflexivity of a text on a painting depicting a tapestry that describes an interior state through allusion to textualized myth (Rapunzel, Arachne, Philomela and

Procne, the Lady of Shalott) is essential. Varo's painting, to use Nancy Miller's term, is a quintessential "arachnology," an inescapable textual web: "Oedipa had looked down at her feet and known, then, because of a painting, that what she stood on had only been woven together a couple thousand miles away in her own tower, was only by accident known as Mexico, and so Pierce had taken her away from nothing, there'd been no escape" (21).[25] The textual web spills out over the frame of Varo's painting and under Oedipa's feet, constituting itself as a magic carpet, a tapestry at least partially of her own embroidery. Oedipa, presumably taken away from the complacencies of southern California by her lover, is taken aback by a painting that tells her the process of fabrication and self-fabrication is continual, or that reminds her she has been taken in by her dream of escape, by her image of herself as the Rapunzel of Kinneret. "What happens, for example," asks Maurice Blanchot, "when one lives an event as an image?" He answers his own question in terms directly applicable to Oedipa's situation: "To live an event as an image is not to remain uninvolved. . . . But neither is it to take part freely and decisively. It is *to be taken:* to pass from the region of the real where we hold ourselves at a distance from things the better to order and use them into that other region where the distance holds us."[26] Caught up in a web of her own weaving, in an ecstasy of discovery and reordering, Oedipa passes almost imperceptibly from fabricator to fabrication; she is taken into her desiring machine and lost.

Tedium

What tends to be forgotten in these ecstasies of plotting is the way in which the game, assiduously played, masks its own tedium, its hyper-redundancy. It is a game, ultimately, less of signs than of graphisms, a muted discourse running along the surface of the increasingly insubstantial things among which Oedipa wanders, not surprisingly, lost amid the silence of the signals. In a recent article, Marc Redfield uses Jameson's comment on the postmodern sublime – noting Jameson's insight that one effect of postmodern narrative is to imagine the world as "a rush of filmic images without density" – as a point of departure for a carefully argued discussion of Pynchon's narrative strategies.[27] In his discussion of *V.*, Redfield shifts from the filmic to the theatrical metaphor, suggesting that, "[t]he clenched drama between rudimentary agents or subjects that marks the narcissistic scenario attains theatrical re-enactment as the possibility or condition of Stencil's 'narcissism,' which, in the logic of this fiction, is the possibility or condition of the fiction itself."[28] Redfield's perception strikes me as elegant, and absolutely correct not only in relation to *V.* but to *The Crying of Lot 49* as well. What I wish to note here, however, is the striking affinity of the images (film, theater) and their relation to the concept of narcissism as conditioned by the "logic" of fiction. Such terms can be derived, in a luxuriant specularity, directly from Pynchon's own obsessions: Oedipa's seduction by the ex-child actor "Baby Igor" Metzger upon her arrival in San Narciso is emblematic of the novel's incipient narcissism. The game goes on. Just as Oedipa Maas borrows images from a Remedios Varo tapestry (the metaphor of her own life, really) to read the hypothetical Tristero, so too Redfield borrows from Jameson – but also, initially, from Pynchon – to read Pynchon. The reflexive or narcissistic play of textual repetition is akin to the "automotive incest," the redundant exchange of essentially empty identical items intuited by a horrified Mucho Maas in the sign of N.A.D.A./nada; this reflexivity or redundancy enacts what Borges would signal with approbation as the tedium of game.

It is no coincidence that the graphic sign of the Tristero/W.A.S.T.E. system is a muted, silenced horn. A rigorously flat, obliterated language – the ciphers of N.A.D.A. or W.A.S.T.E. – is dissected through the machinations of the literary detective's desire for meaning. These graphisms disguise both *something*, if only the waste and rubbish of a postmodern society, and *nothing* at all: they are silent, empty signifiers. They carry no message, but represent, fitfully and inconsistently, the binaries of falsity and truth, the script for both the actor and the "real" housewife. N.A.D.A., W.A.S.T.E., and the hieroglyphic graphism of the horn describe the continually changing surface of fragmentary repetition and rarefied reproduction, the unspeakable words that exist only as repeated sound (paradoxically, immutably silenced) in Oedipa's "world."

Frequently, at the level of syntax, Pynchon makes use of convoluted phrasings and carefully staged precautionary rituals to elaborate repetitions that, in their very insistence, act as attenuating factors decrying the concrete existence established in the statements just made. He substitutes instead a reproductive matrix, what in a computer would be a self-replicating virus, which spins out its hopelessly flawed duplications into a muted, improbable void of endlessly redundant supposition. The model is a variation on a logical impossibility: the anti-sentence, framed ambivalently in the schematic representation "X-not is not X." The opening paragraph of Chapter 3 suffices to set the pattern, repeated throughout the novel with the insistence that marks a Borgesian tedium:

> Things then did not delay in turning curious. If one object behind her discovery of what she was to label the Tristero System or often only The Tristero (as if it might be something's secret title) were to bring to an end her encapsulation in her tower, then that night's infidelity with Metzger would logically be the starting point for it; logically. That's what would come to haunt her most, perhaps: the way it fitted, logically, together. As if (as she'd guessed that first minute in San Narciso) there were revelation in progress all around her. (44)

"Things then did not delay in turning curious": the curious awkwardness of this opening sentence calls attention to itself, forcing the reader back over it once again. "Things": a loaded word, since one of the most curious aspects of this curious novel lies in the degree to which the silent presence of tangible objects is persistently undermined, not only "then," at that moment, but continually, from the title page of the novel to the final page with its promise of a revelation still withheld from the reader at the auctioneer's clearing of his throat. Although the mystery revolving around the history and present status of the underground communications systems is "solved," and the crowding revelations do indeed reveal, contrary to expectations, that the Tristero is in fact "something's secret title" (or is it, since the "something" exists only vaguely as a second-level corrupted text within a text?), at the same time the novel manages to suggest that no logically construable explanation for its resolution is possible. However,

Oedipa's repetition of the word "logically" until it becomes almost a mantra chanted to stave off the creeping infection of illogic ("that night's infidelity with Metzger would *logically* be the starting point for it; *logically*. That's what would come to haunt her most, perhaps: the way it fitted, *logically*, together") already reminds us how easily the appeal to logic enigmatically tips into its opposite. We are forced beyond the logical endpoint; we are shown that it is necessary, in J. Hillis Miller's words, "to go even further, even though one might not want to go any further in the direction that 'further' goes."[29] In Pynchon, this movement is intensified when we don't have an inkling of where "further" is taking us, if anywhere at all, or when we suspect "further" of hiding another treacherous conspiracy, if only to mask its necessary illusion. Are we being taken in, or taken for a ride on another circular track through the space without boundaries of the postmodern universe? According to David Seed, in this novel "text leads into text in a way which explains retrospectively why . . . texts and sources recede into each other apparently without end, stretching towards resolution but never reaching it."[30] In any case, the structuring of meaning from chance clues reflects not the (disputable) order of the world but the ordering process of the individual mind. In this process, we recognize the interplay between participation in and alienation from a fascinating, redundant game, played "as if there were revelation in progress," but remaining poised on the necessary uncertainty of the grammatical tense of the subjunctive verb.

I began with an epigraph from Jorge Luis Borges; – the final sentences of his essay on Zeno's second paradox, "Avatars of the Tortoise." The infinitely receding frames of Seed's hypothesized text recall the inverted infinity of Zeno's paradox, in which Achilles, who has given the turtle a handicap of ten paces, is mathemagically unable to recapture a lead in the fractional infinity stretching between zero and one. The paradox of the infinite regression, whose resolution seems so absurdly obvious to a thinker using common sense, represented an insoluble problem for almost two thousand years until the construction of irrational numbers allowed thinkers to fill in the infinitesimal gaps between the infinite fractions, creating the mathematics of a temporal continuum. I would like to end, then, with the first sentences of that same essay, Borges's "revelation in progress": "Hay un concepto que es el corruptor y el desatinador de los otros. No hablo del Mal cuyo limitado imperio es la ética; hablo del infinito. Yo anhelé compilar alguna vez su móvil historia" ("There is a concept that is the corruptor and distorter of the others. I am not speaking of Evil, whose limited empire is ethics; I am speaking of the infinite. I desired to compile some time its mobile history.")[31] Pynchon's novel is another chapter in that mobile history, and this essay perhaps a footnote appended to the study of the aesthetics of the infinite game.

NOTES

1. Jorge Luis Borges, *Otras inquisiciones* (Buenos Aires: Emecé, 1960): "We (or the indivisible divinity that operates in us) have dreamed the world. We have dreamed it resistant, mysterious, ubiquitous in space and firm in time, but we have allowed in its architecture tenuous and eternal interstices of irrationality so as to know that it is false" (p. 156; my translation).

2. Both articles were originally published in the *Atlantic Monthly*. "The Literature of Exhaustion" appeared in vol. 220 (August 1967): 29–34, and has been much anthologized since; "The Literature of Replenishment" appeared in vol. 245 (January 1980): 65–71.

3. John Updike, "The Author as Librarian," *The New Yorker* 41 (30 October 1965): 245.

4. These citations appear, respectively, in *Ficciones* (Buenos Aires: Emecé, 1956), pp. 11, 143, 143, 162; and in *Otras inquisiciones,* pp. 9, 10, 256.

5. Stephen Hawking, *A Brief History of Time* (New York: Bantam, 1988), p. 136.

6. Borges, *Ficciones,* p. 79.

7. Georgianna M. Colville, *Beyond and Beneath the Mantle: On Thomas Pynchon's "The Crying of Lot 49"* (Amsterdam: Rodolphi, 1988), p. 14.

8. *Ficciones,* pp. 89, 95.

9. Tony Tanner, *Thomas Pynchon* (New York: Methuen, 1982), p. 22.

10. In the best postmodern fashion, Pynchon has also included in the text a parody of the overeager overinterpreter in Professor Bortz, the Wharfinger expert: "But should Bortz have exfoliated the mere words so lushly, into such unnatural roses, under which, in whose

red, scented dusk, dark history slithered unseen?" (163). The lush exfoliation of Pynchon's own prose in this passage is very much to the point.

11. Colville, *Beyond and Beneath the Mantle*, p. 27.
12. Michel Foucault, *The Order of Things* (New York: Vintage, 1970), p. 118.
13. Roland Barthes, *S/Z: An Essay*, trans. Richard Miller (New York: Hill & Wang, 1974), p. 76.
14. Michael Holquist, "Whodunit and Other Questions: Metaphysical Detective Stories in Postwar Fiction," in *The Poetics of Murder: Detective Fiction and Literary Theory*, ed. Glenn E. Most and William Stowe (New York: Harcourt Brace Jovanovich, 1983), p. 157.
15. Geoffrey Hartman, "Literature High and Low: The Case of the Mystery Story," in Most and Stowe, eds., *The Poetics of Murder*, p. 225.
16. Tanner, *Thomas Pynchon*, p. 20–2.
17. Alain Robbe-Grillet, *For a New Novel: Essays on Fiction*, trans. Richard Howard (New York: Grove Press, 1965), p. 188.
18. Fredric Jameson, "On Raymond Chandler," in Most and Stowe, eds., *The Poetics of Murder*, p. 123.
19. J. Hillis Miller, "Figure in Borges's 'Death and the Compass': Red Scharlach as Hermeneut," *Dieciocho* 10 (1987): 58.
20. The term derives from Heath's discussion of mid-century French fiction in his book *The Nouveau Roman: A Study in the Practice of Writing* (Philadelphia: Temple University Press, 1972), p. 136.
21. Brian McHale, *Pöstmödernist Fiction* (New York: Methuen, 1987), p. 24.
22. Jacques Derrida, *The Margins of Philosophy*, trans. Alan Bass (Chicago: University of Chicago Press, 1972), p. 222.
23. Consider, as Borges does, the vast difference in the variant readings of an imaginary novel by Herbert Quain, *April March* (the novel that provoked his observation on the nature of the literary game): "Hasta el nombre es un débil *calembour:* no significa *Marcha de abril* sino literalmente *Abril marzo*" ("Even the title is a weak *calembour:* it does not mean *The March* [in either sense] *of April* [or, we might add, the proper name "April March"] but rather, literally, [the months] *April March*" (*Ficciones*, p. 79); that is, it signals only the backwards march of time: sixty-one days' worth, to be exact.
24. Jorge Luis Borges, *El hacedor* (Buenos Aires: Emecé, 1960), pp. 155–6.
25. Miller defines the arachnology as:
    a critical positioning which reads *against* the weave of indifferentiation to discover the embodiment in writing of a gendered subject; to recover within

representation the emblems of its construction. . . . In the neologism of the text as hyphology, the mode of production is privileged over the subject, whose supervising identity is dissolved in the web. But Arachne's story . . . is not only the tale of a text as tissue: it evokes a bodily substance and a violence to the teller that is not adequately accounted for by a torn web. (Nancy K. Miller, *Subject to Change: Reading Feminist Writing* [New York: Columbia University Press, 1988], pp. 80, 82)

It would be tangential to this project to read Varo's paintings in this respect.

26. Maurice Blanchot, *The Space of Literature,* trans. Ann Smock (Lincoln: University of Nebraska Press, 1982), p. 261; my emphasis.

27. Fredric Jameson, "Postmodernism: or, The Cultural Logic of Late Capitalism," *New Left Review* 146 (1984): 77.

28. Marc Redfield, "Pynchon's Postmodern Sublime," *PMLA* 104 (1989): 158.

29. Miller, "Figure in Borges's 'Death and the Compass,'" p. 59.

30. David Seed, *The Fictional Labyrinths of Thomas Pynchon* (Iowa City: University of Iowa Press, 1989), p. 127.

31. Borges, *Otras inquisiciones,* p. 149.

3

Toward the Schizo-Text:
Paranoia as Semiotic Regime in
The Crying of Lot 49

JOHN JOHNSTON

I

FIRST and foremost, Thomas Pynchon's second novel, *The Crying of Lot 49*, is concerned with signs and their "reading" or interpretation. This would seem to be an obvious constant in Pynchon's fiction. In his first novel, *V.*, signs proliferate – above all, the letter V and the V-shape – as one of the major characters, Herbert Stencil, attempts to link the appearances of a mysterious woman with episodes of violence and decadence in the history of the twentieth century. In *Gravity's Rainbow,* the central character, Tyrone Slothrop, as well as many of the minor characters are particularly adept at reading signs – not only shapes in the sky but mandalas, whip scars, reefers, trout guts, and Tarot cards amid a whole spectrum of semiotic material. *The Crying of Lot 49* differs from these two much longer flanking novels in that its focus is confined to the experience of one character, Oedipa Maas, or rather, to a kind of specific reading and interpretation of signs that for the moment we can simply call "paranoia." In reading the novel, however, we are compelled to consider paranoia less as a mental aberration than as a specific "regime of signs," that is, as a basic type of organization of signs in which the semiotic or signifying potential is dominant.[1]

A basic postulate of semiotics is that signs refer to other signs. Thus the first question is not what a given sign signifies, but to which other signs it refers, or which signs add themselves to it to form an endless network that projects its shadow onto an amorphous atmospheric continuum. In the beginning, as the anthropologist Claude Lévi-Strauss tells it, there was a delirious proliferation of signs; suddenly, the world began to signify, before anyone knew *what* it signified.[2] But what initiates the process of signification? Clearly something must start it off, an object or event must detach itself from a vague or indistinct background and begin to appear as a mysteriously meaningful "sign," all while withholding its exact meaning. However, only when a number of different signs begin to refer to one another and thus link up "logically," or otherwise form an apparently meaningful configuration, does interpretation seem to be called for.

It is just this sudden proliferation of signs that characterizes Oedipa Maas's experience in *The Crying of Lot 49.* The novel begins with Oedipa being drawn out of her ordinary northern California suburban life in order to execute Pierce Inverarity's will. The early chapters chart her gradual "sensitizing" to the feeling that "revelation [was] in progress all around her" (44). This feeling is initiated when she first enters San Narciso, the center of Inevarity's vast and tangled holdings, a realm that "was less an identifiable city than a grouping of concepts – census tracts, special purpose bond-issue districts, shopping nuclei, all overlaid with access roads to its own freeway" (24). It is against this atmospheric, relatively indistinct background ("if there was any vital difference between it and the rest of Southern California, it was invisible on first glance") that Oedipa's first "sensitizing" will take place. As she drives slowly down the slope overlooking San Narciso, she experiences an "odd, religious instant" when the "vast sprawl of houses" recalls her first glimpse of the printed circuit of a transistor radio:

> The ordered swirl of houses and streets, from this high angle, sprang at her now with the same unexpected, astonishing clarity as the circuit card had. Though she knew even less about radios than about Southern Californians, there were to both outward patterns a hieroglyphic sense of concealed meaning, of an intent to communicate. There'd seemed no limit to what the printed circuit could have told her (if she had tried to find out); so in her first minute of San Narciso, a revelation trembled just past the threshold of understanding. Smog hung all round the horizon, the sun on the bright beige countryside was painful; she and the Chevy seemed parked at the centre of an odd, religious instant. As if, on some other frequency, or out of the eye of some whirlwind rotating too slow for her heated

skin even to feel the centrifugal coolness of, words were being spoken. (24–5)

Later, while watching a movie on television with Metzger, her co-executor and soon-to-be-lover, Oedipa again experiences an "immediacy" and "some promise of hierophany" (31) when an advertisement for Fangoso Lagoons, one of Inverarity's housing developments, flashes onto the screen.

What is striking, in both instances, is the obvious gap between the seeming banality of the "contents" of Oedipa's perception and the religious imagery of revelation that it evokes. In both cases, the association between the medium of electronic communication and "words" that might offer "promise of hierophany" is resonant but also culturally disjunctive. No doubt some readers might take the episodes as the first evidence that Oedipa is possibly "crazy," since only "crazy" people hear voices no one else hears or respond to the promise of religious revelation in the total absence of a meaningful context. Furthermore, Pynchon's text itself seems shyly reticent about the nature of these incipient revelations, as if operating in the mode of "ritual reluctance," which for Oedipa will characterize the staging of the seventeenth century revenge tragedy she later sees, where it is hinted that certain words will not be spoken, and certain things will not be seen or represented directly. A stronger reading of the passages, however, might suggest that Oedipa's "sensitizing" is an instance of uncanny repetition, in the Freudian sense of defamiliarizing the familiar. The aerial view of San Narciso not only *resembles* a transistor circuit board but *repeats* an earlier experience which may not be directly accessible to consciousness. The television experience in turn repeats the earlier one with an expansion of associations (water, human bones, the *Book of the Dead*).

But perhaps what is most uncanny, and what Oedipa responds to almost subliminally, is the sudden birth of the sign itself according to an odd but clearly emergent pattern: something familiar repeats itself, but with a noticeable difference, deviation, or deformation. The experience on the slope repeats an earlier one, but in a totally different setting; the television commercial repeats the second, but again with marked differences of detail. The name of the city itself follows a pattern: "San Narciso" repeats while differing from the name of another city, San Francisco. It also echoes the name Narcissus (a "Saint Narcissus" will later be mentioned in the play), but in either case the effect is the same. It is according to this pattern of repetition with a difference, of an echo and distortion producing an oscillation between identity and difference, that signs in the novel will be distinguishable *as* signs. In this sense the sign possesses a structural ambiguity: it points toward a presumed referent, but at the same time deflects us toward another sign. According to the same logic, Oedipa's own name will obtrude as a sign, since it both echoes and differs from "Oedipus." A second echo and distortion of the name will occur when Oedipa's husband Mucho pronounces it "Edna Mosh" (139) in order to offset the distorting effects of a radio transmission. In a somewhat humorous inversion (and further confirmation) of the special semiotic logic at work in the novel, the transmission will thus convert her name *as* sign back into a mere ordinary name.[3]

As Oedipa herself notes, "[t]hings did not delay in turning curious" (44) after her "sensitizing." What she means, of course, is that against this relatively undifferentiated California landscape signs begin to detach themselves and proliferate with an ambiguous, insistent, and even seductive logic. Oedipa finds such signs – like the sign of the partially exposed nymph beckoning above Echo Courts – irresistible, partly because they somehow seem intended for *her*, or to address her directly: "The face of the nymph's was much like Oedipa's, which didn't startle her so much as a concealed blower system that kept the nymph's gauze chiton in constant agitation, revealing enormous vermillion-tipped breasts and long pink thighs at each flap" (26). Retrospectively, the motel sign may suggest that the reader is to view sexual seduction as a parody of revelation, especially since soon after its appearance Oedipa herself is seduced by Metzger. The game of Strip Botticelli that Oedipa plays that evening with Metzger – a game which, not incidentally, requires the gradual revelation of the flesh in accordance with the reading and interpretation of signs or "clues" in a Hollywood film – strongly indicates that "the revelation . . . in progress all around her" may also be a seduction. When Oedipa discovers, after having already paid the penalty for losing the bet (sex with Metzger), that she actually won, she asks Metzger what Pierce had told him about her. "'That you wouldn't be easy'" (43) is Metzger's direct reply, thus suggesting that his seduction of Oedipa was always assumed by both men and would therefore lend weight to the possibility that the execution of Pierce's will may indeed be part of a larger seduction planned by the dead man. As many readers will also notice, Oedipa's "peculiar seduction" by Metzger, as she terms it, is linked to a complex pattern of sexual imagery (Oedipa will later feel "pregnant with something"). But the point to be emphasized here is simply that reading signs (looking for revelation) and being seduced are closely related at the outset. Given that signs themselves possess a seductive power, it should not be surprising that signs may be used to seduce.

Interpretation seems to be called for when constellations of signs begin to refer to one another in a manner not readily explainable in the codes of public or conventional systems of meaning. As in the case of Oedipa's experience, these signs can be quite diverse and heterogeneous in nature, as long as they are clearly marked *as* signs. A flawed U.S. postage stamp, a visual symbol (the "muted" post horn) scrawled on a bathroom wall, human bones at the bottom of a lake, mysterious lines from a seventeenth century revenge tragedy traced to a "corrupt" text: all are "signs" according to the pattern defined above. Now, not only do such signs proliferate, as indicative of their character as signs, but they also refer to each other, at least for Oedipa, by seeming to point to a master or unifying sign which she comes to call Tristero. In short, these signs can all be explained if Oedipa assumes that, operating in contemporary California, there is a secret or underground mail system with a complex history reaching back to origins in the political conflicts of northern Europe during the Renaissance. Oedipa's efforts to discover whether these and other signs actually constitute evidence of the Tristero's existence, or, if not, what this evidence must mean, soon become the armature of the novel's detective plot. Her quest will culminate in four symmetrical possibilities: either she has indeed stumbled onto a secret organization having objective, historical existence by which a number of America's alienated and disenfranchised are communicating; or she is hallucinating it by projecting a pattern onto various signs only randomly associated; or she is the victim of a hoax set up by Inverarity, possibly as a means of perpetuating himself beyond death; or she is hallucinating such a hoax, in a semiosis of the second possibility. The novel concludes with these four possibilities intact as Oedipa awaits the revelation of the auctioneer's cry at the beginning of the sale of a collection of stamps, those "frankings" of specific communicative acts.

Although this last scene contains various signs that might tend to confirm one or another of these four possibilities, the reader is left, like Oedipa, dangling just this side of the heralded revelation. Because the narrator refuses the reader any view superior to Oedipa's, many readers will assume that Oedipa internalizes to a certain extent their own roles as readers. Thus her quest to un-cover the reality and meaning of the Tristero dramatizes the read-er's attempt to decipher and make sense of the various signs that proliferate through the novel, as if its texture, like the California landscape, were communicating on several levels. But if the signs in *The Crying of Lot 49* are haunting and ambiguous for its main character, they are no less uncertain for the reader, who must assume the position of interpreter. For example, as mentioned earlier, Oedipa's name evokes the renowned riddle-solver of Greek tragedy, whose quest to discover the cause of the Theban plague leads to the revelation that he himself is the culprit he seeks. Does the Oedipus story provide a pattern for interpreting the signs in Pynchon's novel, or is it only an ambiguous, possibly deceptive invitation planted by the author? The same question can be asked about other patterns, notably the references to Maxwell's Demon and information theory, or to the Pentecost and "speaking in tongues."[4] These patterns are clearly "there" in the text, not the projections of various readers. The question, however, is what do they ultimately mean? Obviously they enrich the novel's surface, giving it a densely layered significance; but do they provide a privileged access to its "meaning"? But before we can ask such a question, especially about a novel so concerned with signs and the processes of signification, we must first determine the nature of the structure that makes interpretation possible.

As a first step toward understanding the novel's foregrounding of semiotic processes, let us consider Oedipa's "sensitizing" from a somewhat different perspective. For there is another pattern established at the novel's outset, which has to do with her status as an interpreter, and perhaps with the ultimate significance of her name. Chapter 1 concludes with a long summary paragraph about the significance of Oedipa's affair with Inverarity, and about what, for Oedipa, "remained yet had somehow, before this, stayed away" (20). This rather vague background feeling is not so much defined as illustrated by the short ensuing narrative that summarizes their relationship. Before Pierce, Oedipa's life had been buffered, insulated, marked by an absence of intensity, as if she were a prisoner held magically in a tower and Pierce had come to rescue her. But Inverarity had only seemed to rescue her, for "all that had then gone on between them had never really escaped the confinement of that tower" (20). This revelation had come to Oedipa in Mexico City, while standing before the triptych entitled "Bordando el Manto Terrestre" by the Spanish exile Remedios Varo. For Oedipa the painting's depiction of captive maidens who have embroidered a huge tapestry that spills out of the tower's windows and fills the world (or rather, *is* the world, for everything outside the tower is part of the tapestry) signifies her own plight: she is still a captive herself, and "her tower, its height and architecture, are like her ego only incidental . . . what really keeps her where she is is magic, anonymous and malignant, visited on her from outside and for no reason at all" (21). Armed with only "gut fear and female cunning," she asks herself, what can she possibly do: "she may fall back on superstition, or take up a useful hobby like embroidery, or go mad, or marry a disk jockey" (22).

When the novel opens Oedipa has already made the last choice, and when it concludes she will find herself again confronting a quadruple array of possibilities. The passage is therefore striking for the way it mirrors symmetrically the set of possibilities she is left with at the novel's end. But if this internal duplication frames the novel's plot, it also raises its central question – namely, has Oedipa's pursuit of the Tristero finally brought her out of the tower and into confrontation with something outside, something truly Other? If so, the consequences are fully apparent. For if her quest has simply been the mechanism of her more elaborate seduction by Inverarity, both her identity and meaning itself are conserved.

But if the Tristero figures or stands for some radical otherness or difference, or some limit of the meaningful, then not only is Oedipa's identity in question, but "meaning" by definition becomes problematic. In either case, representation – the relationship between words or signs and what they supposedly designate – is completely uncertain, since it either functions deceptively or is fundamentally inadequate.

Facing such uncertainty, we may well wonder how to answer this basic plot question. The key would seem to lie, if anywhere, in the series of men with whom Oedipa is brought into contact in the course of her quest, since it is only through them that she arrives at any sense of what the Tristero is. At the beginning of Chapter 3, Oedipa herself makes the initial connection: "If one object behind her discovery of what she was to label the Tristero System or often only the Tristero (as if it might be something's secret title) were to bring to an end her encapsulation in her tower, then that night's infidelity with Metzger would logically be the starting point for it; logically" (44). However, Oedipa seems to sense from the outset that there is more than just a coincidental relationship between Tristero and the men in her life. Early in her quest she remarks that many of the revelations about the Tristero would come from Pierce's stamp collection, which was often his "substitute" for her. And later, in a passage again alluding to the tower, with Oedipa now in the full grip of her obsession with the Tristero, she will acutely register the gradual disappearance of "her" men: "They are stripping from me, she said subvocally – feeling like a fluttering curtain in a very high window, moving up then out over the abyss – they are stripping away, one by one, my men" (152–3). Thus it should not be surprising that Oedipa will count as her first sensitizing "her peculiar seduction" by Metzger, nor that "[i]t got seriously underway, this sensitizing, either with the letter from Mucho or the evening she and Metzger drifted into a strange bar known as The Scope" (45). It is in The Scope that Oedipa first witnesses mail being delivered by what appears to be a secret or alternative mail system, and where she first encounters the sign of the Tristero, the muted post horn. But The Scope is also where she meets Mike Fallopian, another man in the expanding series of men who becomes essential to her quest. In fact, for each clue or "sign" of the Tristero's existence there is also an associated male character, making it possible to trace the novel's plot as a series of encounters Oedipa has with different male characters, each of whom bears a sign of Tristero's existence, or embodies an interpretive stance with direct implications about its existence.

The crucial point is simply that Oedipa encounters not only a series of signs she is obliged to decipher, but also a series of men whose role in the novel is hardly less important. I want to suggest that these two series – of men and of signs – are not only related but articulate a structure defined by the "resonance" of the two series. More precisely, Oedipa's quest for the meaning of the Tristero System brings about an indeterminate but resonant relationship between a series of men, each of whom defines or represents a subject position (or set of attitudes) in relation to interpretation, and a series of signs to be interpreted which proliferate during her search. As we shall see, the relationship or state of "resonance" between the series of signs and the series of men brought about by Oedipa's search both constitutes the novel's structure and characterizes a particular "semiotic regime." It is in terms of these series that I want to explore the question of why this intersubjective structure cannot include Oedipa, except at the price of her sanity. In essence, Oedipa occupies the "blind spot" in the structure, the point of its articulation and self-effacement; and this is indeed the significance of her name. Once this is understood, we shall be in a position to explore the status of "paranoia" as the novel's incarnation of a specific semiotic regime. In semiotic terms, the novel's "meaning" will turn out to be a function of how this regime requires "interpretation," not as an extrinsic act that stands in secondary or subordinate relation to a more primary experience, but as an intrinsic, even constituent part of that experience.

II

In relation to the series of men Oedipa encounters in the course of the novel, Pierce Inverarity clearly occupies an ambiguous place. As the "first" man in her life (at least as far as we know), he both stands outside the series and may even be considered its "cause," inasmuch as it is his death that initiates her search. Pierce's "pres-

ence" in the novel is therefore both ubiquitous and vague or indeterminate. Not accidentally, Pierce's name evokes the name of the
American founder of semiotics, C. S. Peirce. Appropriately, he
seems to stand behind, to "figure" as it were, one of the novel's
central motifs: that the dead never really go away or disappear, but
persist as "signs."[5] Perhaps it is not so strange, then, that we know
very little about him, except that he speaks in different voices.
Early in the novel, just after Oedipa receives the letter notifying her
of Pierce's death and her appointment as executrix of his will, she
thinks back to the last time she had heard from him, a long-
distance telephone call in which, curiously, he never spoke in his
own voice but modulated from one comic parody to another. This
fracturing of what we assume to be a single individual's voice into
a multiplicity of voices may suggest, among many things, that
Pierce has no single identity or that as a mimic he functions here as
the author's comic double or stand-in. But surely the most com-
pelling interpretation would seek to link this first appearance of
Pierce's voice(s) with the pattern of other telephone calls that
come (as does Pierce's) in the night. Just after the novel opens,
Oedipa receives a late-night call from her psychotherapist, Dr. Hilarious, who "sounded like Pierce doing a Gestapo officer" (16).
And late in the novel, as Oedipa muses on the "American code in
Inverarity's testament," she thinks of

> the voices before and after the dead man's that had phoned at
> random during the darkest, slowest hours, searching ceaseless
> among the dial's ten million possibilities for that magical Other who
> would reveal herself out of the roar of relays, monotonous litanies
> of insult, filth, fantasy, love whose brute reputation must someday
> call into being the trigger for the unnameable act, the recognition,
> the Word. (180)

The logic connecting these passages is indeed peculiar, like the
earlier conjunction of electronic communication and the imma-
nence of revelation; it is as if Pierce's death somehow made the
"promise of hierophany" by electronic communication more likely or necessary. Or is it simply that the instantaneousness of voice
transmission by electronic media, what Marshall McLuhan called
"the miracle of secular communication," so closely resembles, perhaps even parodies, the reception of the divine *logos?* Whatever the

case, let us note that unlike the other men Oedipa encounters, Pierce is not so much an interpreter as an emitter of signs.

Hernando Joaquin de Tristero y Calavera, the putative founder of the Tristero, occupies an equally ambiguous place in the series. For one thing, his very historical reality is a matter of uncertainty. As a figure pieced together from references Oedipa unearths in obscure and possibly forged historical texts provided by the philatelist Genghis Cohen and the English professor Emory Bortz, Tristero y Calavera may be only a fabrication in which Oedipa unwillingly participates. However, if her work of historical construction is not deceived, and this elusive and mysterious figure actually existed, the consequences are profound. For in this case another series opens up – vertical and temporal, as it were – that would include the actual members of the Tristero, from its beginnings in Brussels in 1577 to its immigration to the U.S. in the 1840s to its appearance in contemporary California. This series would also include the mysterious "book-bidder" who plans to attend the auctioning of Pierce's stamp collection, and possibly Loren Passerine, the auctioneer. Furthermore, if the Tristero series is indeed "real," then the two series would intersect at the novel's conclusion, and Oedipa's revelation would occur precisely at their meeting point. Since we do not know if or how this event will take place, such an intersection remains only a possibility; thus Calavera, or his contemporary representatives, stands at the end of the series, just as Pierce stands at the beginning. In regard to Oedipa's quest, Calavera is the *terminus ad quem*, just as Pierce is the *terminus ab quo*. Furthermore, like Pierce, Calavera is not only dead but also seems to have had indeterminate, multiple identities: "perhaps a madman, perhaps an honest rebel, according to some only a con artist" (157).

Between these two equally uncertain and ambiguous endpoints lies a series of "flesh-and-blood" male characters. Essentially the novel's plot enacts a series of encounters (sometimes repeated) between Oedipa and each of them: Mucho Maas, Metzger, Mike Fallopian, Manny Di Presso, Randolph Driblette, Stanley Koteks, Mr. Thoth, Genghis Cohen, John Nefastis, the member of Inamorati Anonymous she meets at the Greek Way, Jesús Arrabal, the dying sailor, Dr. Hilarius, Winthrope Tremaine, and Emory

Bortz. To say that these encounters constitute the novel's episodic plot and that, together, they may even add up to Oedipa's "seduction" or "debuffering" is not, however, enough. What is most important is that each of these men positions himself as an interpreter of some kind of semiotic material and thereby throws some light on Oedipa's search. In other words, these characters function as what Henry James termed "reflectors." But unlike a typically Jamesian narrative situation in which the reflectors clarify the centralized vision of the protagonist by providing more limited and contrasting viewpoints, here the reflectors provide only decentered and displaced perspectives that cannot be brought back into any centralized alignment. If James's reflectors thus become the means of modeling a view that encompasses and includes – indeed, seem to expand – a "normative" view, Pynchon's characters perform in the opposite manner. As a series of reflectors who are actually refractors, they project a series of wholly divergent views and preclude the possibility of a normative vision. In this sense, *The Crying of Lot 49* articulates a multiplicity, and refuses to resolve itself into a single view that the various minor characters could endorse or support.[6]

Oedipa's husband, Wendell "Mucho" Maas, the first in the series, also occupies a curious double position, insofar as he is both the husband she leaves behind in order to go on her search and one of the men she will later encounter during that search. Mucho's life falls into three stages: his early life as an anguished used car salesman; his life as a disk jockey for a pop music station; and his life as an explorer of the subliminal world of LSD-influenced perception. These three stages correspond to three distinguishable "readings" of signs. As Oedipa remarks, Mucho is too "sensitive" for the first stage: hyper-aware of the "signs" of the stereotypical used car salesman's appearance, of "signs" like sawdust that raise the suspicions of potential buyers, and of the cars themselves as "signs" of the customer's identity, Mucho constantly frets over a job emblematized by the N.A.D.A. sign (for National Automobile Dealers' Association) that speaks to him in his nightmares: "Just this creaking metal sign that said nada, nada, against the blue sky" (144). From this landscape of alienation Mucho moves into the McLuhanesque world of electronic media, where he becomes an interpreter (and sometimes the recipient) of the signs of adolescent sexual desire, a development that stands at the beginning of Oedipa's quest.

When Oedipa encounters Mucho later in the novel, just after Dr. Hilarius has flipped out and Mucho arrives on the scene to report the event, she quickly discerns that there is something odd about his behavior. As his boss, Funch, explains, Mucho is losing his identity: he has become less himself and more a generic person, a "walking assembly" of voices. When Oedipa discovers that he has been ingesting regularly the supply of LSD pills that Dr. Hilarius has made available (but which she has refused), all becomes clear. Mucho's interest in doing "spectrum analysis" in his head, which entails breaking down audible sounds into units that lie below the threshold of the socially meaningful, is for Oedipa a retreat into a kind of sensory solipsism; inversely, his recombination of sounds and feelings – his analysis of the phrase "rich, chocolaty good-ness," for example, or the words "she loves you" from a pop song (142–3) – dissolves all coded differences into meaningless gener-ality. The promise of meaning Mucho offers (a wholly secular "hierophany") is simultaneously too far below and above the pub-lic level of coded or significant meaning, effectually denying the signifying character of the sign. Oedipa thus rejects Mucho's ap-peal as an unworthy alternative to her quest for meaning.

It is Metzger, Oedipa's fellow executor and initial marital in-fidelity, who occupies the first relatively unproblematic position in the series of men. Metzger's singularity is that he is both the closest to Inverarity personally (as Inverarity's lawyer, he is in one sense his personal representative) and the least active interpreter of signs. About Metzger we are most vividly aware of the details of his physical appearance. As Pynchon emphasizes in the title of a section of the novel published earlier as a story, Oedipa inhabits the world of the flesh, and this is precisely the level on which she meets Metzger.[7] After seducing Oedipa, he takes remarkably little interest in her quest, and finally abandons her to run off with a sixteen-year-old girl. As the novel's "representative of the entirely profane," according to one critic, Metzger lives in a world made up solely of images; in fact, he often behaves as if he were on cam-era.[8] Although his image can be doubled (as in a Hollywood film, or in the humorous convolutions possible because of his double profession as lawyer and actor), this image never takes on the status of a sign. In a world where there are *only* images (behind the image there are only more images), there is nothing to interpret, no "promise of hierophany." Metzger thus occupies a position – the zero degree of interpretive activity – which figures or represents a flat denial of the "transcendent meaning" that Oedipa seeks.

The more insidious denial proffered by Mike Fallopian proves to be far more serious. When Oedipa first encounters him in The Scope, he is proselytizing for the Peter Pinguid Society, a small "right-wing nut outfit," as Metzger describes it, which communicates via an alternative mail system that may be part of Yoyodyne's interoffice mail system or part of Tristero. An historian of sorts, Fallopian is also writing a book about the history of private mail systems in the U.S., the up and down fortunes of which he interprets as a "parable of power." As Oedipa's investigations unfold he appears initially helpful, pointing out, for example, that Stanley Koteks, the engineer she encounters at Yoyodyne doodling the muted post horn sign and who will lead her to John Nefastis, is "part of some underground" of engineers unhappy with the current system. But Fallopian also comes up with a different, perhaps more historically plausible explanation of Mr. Thoth's story of the masked marauders, dressed in black, who attacked the Pony Express riders in the 1840s. For Oedipa, the details of that story point toward the Tristero, especially since Mr. Thoth possesses a ring bearing the muted post horn which his grandfather, the uncertain "source" of the story, reputedly cut from the finger of one of the attackers. For Fallopian, however, the details suggest that Oedipa is following an "accidental correlation," – and that the marauders were more likely hired by the federal government to suppress the competition.

Returning to The Scope late in the novel for what proves to be her last encounter with Fallopian, Oedipa notices that something is different: when he asks about her quest, the look he gives her is "sympathetic, annoyed, perhaps also a little erotic" (167). Having given him a status report, Oedipa remarks that she is "'surprised that you people aren't using the system too,'" to which Fallopian replies, "'Are we an underground? . . . Are we rejects?'" (167). In rapid succession, Fallopian then suggests three possibilities: "'Maybe we haven't found them yet . . . Or maybe they haven't approached us. Or maybe we are using W.A.S.T.E., only it's a secret'" (167). But then he discloses a fourth possibility: that perhaps Tristero is a hoax, "'something Inverarity set up before he died.'" The exchange turns bitter as Oedipa reacts negatively to an interpretation she herself has already considered but which, like the fact that "someday she would have to die," she does not want to face.

Fallopian's advice to Oedipa bolsters an empirical reading of signs: he suggests that she must verify her sources. Two sources who prove crucial for her quest are Genghis Cohen and Emory Bortz. In contrast to the skeptical, pragmatic Fallopian, they encourage her belief in the Tristero, primarily by providing her with the means to authenticate its historical existence – Cohen by discovering "counterfeit stamps" whose deviations and discrepancies may be signs of the Tristero, and Bortz by supplying textual evidence and a projected history supposedly consistent with the known "facts." Both men appear to be gentleman–scholar types, motivated by intellectual curiosity, with nothing at stake in the quest (thus differing from Fallopian, whose right-wing allegiances become more pronounced in the course of the novel). However, as Oedipa herself must admit, both men can be linked back to Inverarity's estate, and the "scholarly" physical and historical evidence (and interpretations) they produce may well be bogus.

In this succession of empiricist and scholastic modes of interpretation, the most explicit interpreter Oedipa encounters is Randolph Driblette, the director of the Tank Players' production of Richard Wharfinger's *The Courier's Tragedy*, which Oedipa attends early in the novel. According to the work of historical construction Oedipa puzzles out later with Bortz, Wharfinger must have encountered the "Trystero" story (with its variant spelling) in the travelogue of a contemporary, Dr. Diocletian Blobb, who was set upon by a group of brigands dressed in black near the Lake of Piety while traveling through Italy in a Thurn and Taxis mail coach. After murdering everyone but Blobb and his servant, the brigands announced themselves as members of an alternate courier system called the Trystero, ready to do business with the English King and Parliament. In his revenge play, Wharfinger introduces the Trystero as the secret courier system used by the evil Duke Angelo to do what he cannot trust anyone else to do, namely to get rid of the rightful but "disinherited" Niccolo, who has disguised himself as a Thurn and Taxis courier. His murder by the Trystero occurs near the Lake of Piety, where many years before the outlaws had similarly murdered the hand-picked guard of his father, the good Duke, supposedly at Angelo's behest. However, again according to Oedipa and Bortz's work of historical reconstruction, Wharfinger himself apparently did not actually name the Trystero in the lines which initially drew Oedipa's attention. It turns out that the lines in question –

> He that we last as Thurn and Taxis knew
> Now recks no lord but the stiletto's Thorn
> And Tacit lies the gold once-knotted horn.
> No hallowed skein of stars can ward, I trow,
> Who's once been set his tryst with Trystero. (75)

– were probably introduced in a pornographic folio edition printed by members of a radical Puritan group, the "Scurvhamites," in order to damn eternally both play and author. For those putative editors, the Trystero symbolized "the brute Other" (156), or that part of the universe that ran opposite to the will of God: "some opposite principle, something blind, soulless: a brute automatism that led to eternal death" (155). For reasons which Oedipa is never able to track down, the lines in question – at best a textual variant, at worst an unjustifiable or "corrupt" editorial emendation – were published in the unauthorized paperback edition used as Driblette's source for the play's production.

It is within the context of this labyrinth of historical interpretation and textual transformation that Oedipa's encounter with Driblette must be considered. Oedipa searches out Driblette after the performance because she is curious about certain parallels between the human bones of the murdered Lost Guard (used in the play by Angelo to manufacture a miraculous ink) and certain bones in Lake Inverarity – apparently those of U.S. infantrymen killed by Germans in 1943 near Lago di Pieta in Italy and, curiously, purchased by an American company to be converted into filters for cigarettes. Instead, she finds herself asking about the text of the play and the mysterious allusion to the Trystero spoken by Driblette himself (playing Gennaro) in its dramatic conclusion. The encounter with Driblette is essential, then, not only because he is her first direct source of the Tristero as master sign, but also because the encounter itself is dense with implication.

First of all, to her question regarding the source text, Driblette responds by asking, "'Why . . . is everybody so interested in texts?' " (78). The question can imply either that Oedipa is just part of the scholarly dispute surrounding the text, or that Driblette has been asked by someone, for unknown reasons, to pronounce these particular lines for this performance. Moreover, in response to her questions Driblette assumes the same "knowing" look and manner he had coached his cast to give whenever the subject of the Trystero came up. The "look" itself, and the presence of the Trystero assassins on stage in the fourth act, are Driblette's own interpretive emendations to the production. But when Oedipa inquires about this particular emphasis, he responds:

> "You don't understand," getting mad. "You guys, you're like Puritans about the Bible. So hung up with words, words. You know where that play exists, not in that file cabinet [where he keeps the scripts], not in any paperback you're looking at, but −" a hand emerged from the veil of shower-steam to indicate his suspended head − "in here. That's what I'm for. To give the spirit flesh. The words, who cares? They're rote noises to hold line bashes with, to get past the bone barriers around an actor's memory, right? But the reality is in *this* head. Mine. I'm the projector at the planetarium, all the closed little universe visible in the circle of that stage is coming out of my mouth, eyes, sometimes other orifices also." (79)

When Oedipa persists with questions about the Trystero, Driblette responds with a hypothetical assertion: if he were to dissolve and be washed down the drain into the Pacific (here, he anticipates his eventual suicide) all of the play − "that little world" − would also vanish, except for a certain "residue . . . the things Wharfinger didn't lie about . . . but they would be traces, fossils. Dead, mineral, without value or potential" (80). Driblette's last words, framed conditionally but directed personally at Oedipa, oddly conflate falling in love with assuming a role as quester, a role that Oedipa herself will soon undertake:

> "You could fall in love with me, you can talk to my shrink, you can hide a tape recorder in my bedroom, see what I talk about from wherever I am when I sleep. You want to do that? You can put together clues, develop a thesis, or several, about why characters reacted to the Trystero possibility the way they did, why the assassins came on, why the black costumes. You could waste your life that way and never touch the truth. Wharfinger supplied words and a yarn. I gave them life. That's it." (80)

Driblette's words, or rather the interpretive attitude they express, have an immediate impact on Oedipa. Soon after the encounter, thinking about Pierce's will more closely than before, she determines "to bestow life on what had persisted, to try to be what Driblette was, the dark machine in the centre of the planetarium, to bring the estate into pulsing stelliferous Meaning" (82). She admits, however, that too much stands in her way: "her deep ignorance of the law, of investment, of real estate, ultimately of the dead man himself" (82). But in contrast to the block she experiences with Pierce's will, revelations from the Trystero "now seemed to come crowding in exponentially, as if the more she collected the more would come to her, until everything she saw, smelled, dreamed, remembered, would somehow come to be woven into The Tristero" (81). This intensely experienced influx of signs suggests that, in regard to the Tristero, she can never simply assume the position of an interpreter projecting a meaning. Despite both Driblette's advice and the tenuousness of the evidence, she will never relinquish the hope that the Tristero is more than just an assembly of "dead" signs and historical "residue" to which she gives life through her own projection of a world.

Several of the minor characters illustrate with varying degrees of intensity and seriousness this "subjectivist" view of interpretation that Oedipa implicitly rejects. Dr. Hilarius, for example, hallucinates that he is under siege by Israeli agents who are out to get him, although his paranoia is probably justified since he did participate in Nazi death camp atrocities. Although Hilarius clearly serves satirical purposes, he is also used to make a serious plea. When Oedipa reveals that she has come to him to be talked out of a fantasy – she means of course her obsession with the Tristero – Hilarius replies: "'Cherish it! . . . What else do any of you have? Hold it tightly by its little tentacle, don't let the Freudians coax it away or the pharmacists poison it out of you. Whatever it is, hold it dear, for when you lose it you go over by that much to the others. You begin to cease to be'" (138). Hilarius rejects the theories of Freud and Jung and the behaviorists as if they were part of some larger historical or cultural plot – of which the camps were the outward sign – to rob us of our individual identities. In valorizing fantasy as the essential component of individual identity, Hilarius assumes a world in which normative behavior is no longer possible or desirable.

John Nefastis provides one such example of a fantasy that defines his identity, a fantasy in which Oedipa is not able to share. Oedipa visits him at his Berkeley apartment because she thinks he is communicating via the Tristero System and, therefore, may be able to shed light on it. Instead, she finds herself in an extended encounter with Maxwell's Demon. As Oedipa is quick to perceive, there are many analogies between her situation and that of Nefastis, who is as obsessed with the word "entropy" as she is with the Tristero. Nefastis's machine is an updated version of John Clerk Maxwell's speculative heat energy machine. Maxwell postulated that if an intelligence (the "demon," as he called it) could somehow sort hot and cold molecules into opposing chambers, the resulting heat differential could be used as an energy source. What Maxwell didn't know was that the energy required for the sorting would more than offset the energy gained by the machine. In Nefastis's machine this loss is to be made up by an outside observer (the so-called "sensitive") who supplies energy in the form of information which he or she "communicates" to the demon by concentrating on a photograph of Maxwell. This exchange is possible because, as was discovered in the 1930s, the equations for thermodynamic entropy (or heat loss) and entropy in information theory (noise as a measure of disorganization in a system) turn out to be the same. Nefastis's machine is thus based on a spiritualist application of the historical coincidence of two scientific laws. A fundamentalist and true believer, Nefastis takes for an objective truth what is at best a metaphor. His machine requires a "leap of faith" that Oedipa cannot make, though, as she admits to herself, the effect would be "wonderful."

The relation between truth and metaphor also becomes crucial in Oedipa's encounter, after a night of drifting through San Francisco, with the dying sailor who bears the sign of the Tristero, the muted post horn, tattooed on his hand. In a heightened passage which brings together many of the novel's themes, she thinks about "the massive destruction of information" his death will bring. The fact that he suffers from DTs makes her think of the time differential "dt" in calculus and brings her to speculate about the "high magic of low puns." But it is the status of metaphor that knits the passage together:

> Behind the initials [the DTs] was a metaphor, a delirium tremens, a trembling unfurrowing of the mind's plowshare. The saint whose water can light lamps, the clairvoyant whose lapse in recall is the breath of God, the true paranoid for whom all is organized in spheres joyful or threatening about the central pole of himself, the dreamer whose puns probe ancient fetid shafts and tunnels of truth all act in the same special relevance to the word, or whatever it is the word is there, buffering, to protect us from. The act of metaphor then was a thrust at the truth and a lie, depending on where you were: inside, safe, or outside, lost. Oedipa did not know where she was. (128–9)

Earlier in the scene the sailor had asked Oedipa to mail a letter for him, a kind of last testament to his wife, using the Tristero System. The paragraph concludes with Oedipa, having walked for an hour in search of a sign, depositing the letter in a receptacle marked with the initials W.A.S.T.E. Through her act of charity, for a brief moment, Oedipa thus finds herself conscripted as a carrier in the alternative postal system. But the most important effect of the passage is to make us wonder, like Oedipa, what metaphor stands behind the W.A.S.T.E. initials and where she stands – inside or outside – in relation to it. In the language of Nefastis's machine, is she a "sorting Demon" or a "sensitive"?

Although by this point in the novel there appears to be ample evidence that some kind of alternative mail system is functioning in the San Narciso and San Francisco areas, Oedipa's encounters with Nefastis and the dying sailor suggest that the "meaning" of this alternative system (whose sign, W.A.S.T.E., does not necessarily signify the Tristero) depends more on the position, rather than the knowledge, of the observer. Oedipa's encounter with the unnamed member of Inamorati Anonymous in The Greek Way — who also bears the Tristero sign — confirms this point, since he admits to using the system while remaining ignorant of its significance and history. Heightened by the emotional poignancy of her later phone call as "Arnold Snarb" to the same Inamorati, this encounter makes it clear that not only is the network of signs Oedipa calls the Tristero a medium of communication for "isolates," but also that the price of her search for meaning will be her own increasing alienation and solitude. If, as she thinks, the Tristero provides the means by which various "undergrounds" communicate — those politically, socially, and sexually unrecognized in official American life — then, by virtue of their very difference and separateness, they cannot constitute any single existing community that she could somehow join. At best, their various acts of communication represent an "anarchist miracle," as her friend the Mexican anarchist Jesús Arrabal would call it — the silent, almost unrecognizable intrusion of an alien world into the official one.

In each of these encounters with the different male characters — encounters that, taken together, constitute the plot of *The Crying of Lot 49* — Oedipa confronts not only a person but a sign. For whatever the obvious and manifold differences that comprise each encounter, there is always the same triangular structure formed by Oedipa, the male character, and a sign or signs. Oedipa's desire to discover the truth about the Tristero drives the plot forward, but always in relation to a double mediation formed by a series of signs and a series of men. In one way or another, the characters are all interpreters from whom Oedipa hopes to learn how to move from "sign" to "reality." In some episodes the lesson in interpretation occurs only implicitly or through an analogy, as in her encounters with Dr. Hilarius and Nefastis. Yet, with each succeeding encounter, the ultimate reality of the Tristero becomes both more necessary and less certain.

But it also becomes increasingly evident that any direct confrontation with the Tristero, unmediated by signs, would be catastrophic for Oedipa and unrepresentable according to the novel's economy or mode of representation. This structural limit is figured in the imagery of epileptic seizure and mental cauterization. Oedipa herself seems to recognize this limit when she experiences a confluent rush of signs in the offhand comments of Genghis Cohen about the removal of a cemetery for the construction of the San Narciso freeway:

> She could, at this stage of things, recognize signals like that, as the epileptic is said to – an odor, color, pure piercing grace note announcing his seizure. Afterward it is only this signal, really dross, this secular announcement, and never what is revealed during the act, that he remembers. Oedipa wondered whether, at the end of this (if it were supposed to end), she too might not be left with only compiled memories of clues, announcements, intimations, but never the central truth itself, which must somehow each time be too bright for memory to hold; which must always blaze out, destroying its own message irreversibly, leaving an overexposed blank when the ordinary world came back. (95)

In these terms the novel thematizes what from a structural point of view is its own condition of possibility. For if Oedipa's movement toward possible revelation can be characterized as a gradual "stripping" or "de-buffering," then, textually, she always functions as an "overexposed blank," a blind spot or point of articulation through which two heterogeneous series begin to resonate, without ever exactly corresponding. Such a correspondence always remains a possibility, but the revelation it would imply would also entail a collapse or mutation of the novel's fundamental structure of doubt and deferral.

III

We must now try to understand this structure more explicitly. As we've already seen, beginning with Oedipa's "sensitizing," a consistent pattern of imagery of religious revelation is used to thematize the signs of the Tristero. During her night's wandering through San Francisco, she wonders if the "gemlike clues" or signs of the Tristero she encounters "were only some kind of compensation. To make up for her having lost the direct, epileptic Word, the cry that might abolish the night" (118). Why should the signs of the Tristero be a compensation for the *logos*? If one has lost contact with the *logos* or Truth, then she or he lives in a condition in which either there are no signs, or the signs are inevitably ambiguous. But why should these signs now appear with the death of Pierce Inverarity, who is hardly representative of a divine or transcendent order? Indeed, Pierce represents an entirely secular order, for the unity of "San Narciso" is only produced by the demands of corporate capitalism, expressed by Pierce as the need "to keep it bouncing." As a wholly secular order, it is subject to death and entropy, as the metaphor of the bouncing ball suggests. Therefore, as Oedipa interprets it, if Pierce is truly "dead," then there is just "the earth" (181), and the signs don't exist *as* signs. Indeed, at one point late in the novel, finding herself completely isolated and geographically disoriented, Oedipa experiences just this disappearance of the sign: "San Narciso at that moment lost (the loss pure, instant, spherical, the sound of a stainless orchestral chime held among the stars and struck lightly), gave up its residue of uniqueness of her; became a name again, was assumed back into the American continuity of crust and mantle" (177). However, if the signs do exist, and are not explainable as Oedipa's own hallucinations or an elaborate trick played by Inverarity, then they must point to the existence of the Tristero, which would constitute an order of meaning behind the obvious: "Behind the hieroglyphic streets . . . a transcendent meaning" (181). In this case, Oedipa realizes, "she might have found The Trystero anywhere in her Republic" (179).

Thus, if Oedipa's encounters do not bring her closer to actual contact with the Tristero, they do make it clear what such contact would mean: that the signs are all "true," that they link together independent of her own interpretive efforts, and that they possess a transcendent order and validity. But to what "reality" would this signifying system of signs correspond? As Oedipa gradually discovers, it would point to the reality of those alienated from official reality, to the reality of the diverse and unassimilated, the socially, politically, and sexually "unrecognized" of American society – the abnormal, the crazy, the poor. But how could any such grouping be unified, except in the negative unity of their difference? They cannot be, except by an order of signs that remains as ambiguous, heterogeneous, and forever contingent upon other circumstances as they themselves are. But this would imply that their unity can never be anything but putative, the projection of an interpreter who can be but the witness to their disjunctive alienations.

Oedipa functions as just such an interpreter: "Decorating each alienation, each species of withdrawal, as cufflink, decal, aimless doodling, there was somehow always the post horn. She grew so to expect it that perhaps she did not see it quite as often as she later was to remember seeing it" (124–5). The language of this passage should make us wonder: Why should these signs, which "decorate" and, thus, seem redundant, be necessary? Aren't the signs of alienation fully visible in themselves? Another way of raising the question is to ask, who are the spokesmen in the novel for the official reality? In effect, there would seem to be only Oedipa herself, since the only other likely candidate, Pierce Inverarity, is dead. As she later acknowledges, Oedipa has been blind to what official discourse (sanctified reason, approved forms of sanity, the "common sense" of the dominant political order) and its communication channels exclude and repress, even though this other reality has always been present, easy to see "if only she'd looked." Oedipa's previous "buffering" thus takes on a political meaning, and Pierce's inability to rescue her from it is easily explained: the two are defined by and share the same white, male-dominated, middle-class, corporate American "reality."[9] With Pierce's death, however, a segment or corporate chunk is loosened from its moorings, and official reality begins to come apart. In the interstices and cracks of a now increasingly entropic system, what had been invisible and repressed rises to the surface in the form of "signs" heralding the possible emergence of an entirely different order of meaning.[10]

Oedipa's "blindness" is therefore not only structural but thematic. She learns to "see" by apprehending what a series of males see in relation to what she wants to see but is honest enough to remain critical of: an alternative "reality" that is not a private, solipsistic fantasy but one that is shared by a heterogeneous community of other interpreters. But by the very nature of this "reality," it cannot exist apart from her perception of it. One can say, therefore, that Oedipa's "hubris" lies less in her desire to prove the autonomous, objective existence of the Tristero (thus avoiding responsibility for it while, paradoxically, admitting that her participation in the quest has abetted the conspiracy) than in her desire to unify and give a single name and history to something heterogeneous by its very nature. To master the sign is to master the reality, but the very mastery she seeks is the mirror image of official discourse itself – a discourse that cannot allow vagrant signs (or people) to migrate ambiguously through the textual strands and interstices of its social and textual fabric.

In this sense, Oedipa's efforts at interpretation do indeed form a "paranoid" projection which finds no sure confirmation or endorsement in the structural logic of the novel. What this projection does, however, is to confirm and extend the inversion of official discourse which Oedipa's interpretation enacts. It does this very simply by offering no representative of rational, institutionalized thought to counter Oedipa's "paranoid" assertions. The series of male characters Oedipa encounters incarnate a variety of interpretive attitudes or postures, but taken together they exclude the very possibility of a normalizing perspective. All are "crazy" or aberrant or marginal in some crucial way. In fact, the only "representative" of official reason is the one internalized in Oedipa's own critical self-consciousness. But this suggests that there is no *essential* difference between paranoia and the structure of official discourse: the former is always already inscribed within the latter; it simply lacks the latter's customary sanction and institutional authority. Official discourse must be viewed, therefore, as the result of a successful plot, and functions as both its "cover-up" and justification. History, or at least official history, is another name for that successful plot; in other terms, history is always a story told from the point of view of the dominant order, which can contain political differences but not ontological ones. Indeed, this will be an underlying theme in Pynchon's next novel, *Gravity's Rainbow.*

IV

Our analysis of the structure of *The Crying of Lot 49* would thus appear to lead inevitably to the conclusion that paranoia and the official discourse of the dominant cultural order belong to the same "semiotic regime." The novel enacts this regime – one that, in structural terms, allows no escape from interpretation, either for

Oedipa or the reader. For Deleuze and Guattari, who construct a typology of four distinguishable "regimes of signs," the semiotic or signifying regime is merely one type that works in relation to the others.[11] As its name suggests, the signifying regime privileges the sign (or signifier), which in its proliferation and infinite circularity (signs always and only refer to other signs), seems at once excessively meaningful and lacking in precise meaning. To a perceiver, these signs appear to be organized in circles that radiate outward from a center of significance. Given this configuration, it is not surprising that Deleuze and Guattari take a particular religious form of organization – that of the despot–god at the center surrounded by interpreter–priests – as their illustrative model. (Actually, the model is merely one form taken by this particular regime of signs; another is the delusional system that psychiatrists call "paranoia.") The interpreter–priests are not supplementary but a fundamental part of the system, since they "must provide the center with more signifiers to overcome the entropy inherent in the system and to make new circles blossom or replenish the old" (TP 114). Because signs themselves are inherently ambiguous, the priests can do this by isolating a portion of the signified, which is then made to correspond to a sign or group of signs "for which the signified has been deemed suitable, thus making it knowable" (TP 114). In this way, they attempt to overcome the "inadequation" between signifier and signified noted by Lévi-Strauss. Through their acts of interpretation the priests are thus responsible for adding to the syntagmatic axis of the sign (along which signs refer to other signs) a second, paradigmatic axis, along which a "suitable signified" or "meaning" is continually fashioned and refashioned. However, since the system is closed upon itself, and all signs must ultimately be made to refer back to the despot–god at the center, a certain redundancy and deception are inherent in the system:

> A new aspect of deception arises, the deception of the priest: interpretation is carried to infinity and never encounters anything to interpret that is not already itself an interpretation. The signified constantly reimparts the signifier, recharges it or produces more of it. The form always comes from the signifier. The ultimate signified is therefore the signifier itself, in its redundancy or "excess." It is

> perfectly futile to claim to transcend interpretation or even communication through the production of the signifier, because communication and interpretation are what always serve to reproduce and produce the signifier. (TP 114)

Hence, one cannot escape from the orbit of signs or signifiers which demand interpretation but always and only refer to other signs (and, therefore, other interpretations). Furthermore, like the necessity of interpretation (Deleuze and Guattari call it "interpretosis," likening it to a disease), deception is built into the regime of signs as a functional necessity.

In *The Crying of Lot 49*, both Oedipa and the reader are trapped in a semiotic regime of this type; to a great extent, they are victimized by its paranoid–despotic character and the necessity of its interpretation. One by one the series of men Oedipa encounters assume the structural position of the interpreter–priest, who provides a meaning or interpretation of the signs wheeling about her. Since, for Oedipa, these signs must ultimately refer either to the Tristero or to Inverarity, a certain ambiguity or "deception" is intrinsically part of the semiotic regime she inhabits.

Another feature of this regime throws even more light on the peculiar indeterminate relationship between Pierce Inverarity and the Tristero, or rather, upon the structural positions they occupy in the novel. Oedipa's problem, simply put, is that she doesn't know whether the signs she encounters emanate from Pierce or the Tristero. Either the two occupy polar extremes, or one collapses into the other. But what initially appears to be an interpretive problem can also be seen as the enactment of Deleuze and Guattari's semiotic model. In their terms, Oedipa doesn't know which one (Pierce or Tristero) is the despot at the center of the system; however, in the semiotic regime, there are always two opposed figures: that of the *despot* at the center, the master Signifier in person to which all the signs refer and about which they revolve, and his negative mirror-image, the *scapegoat* on the outside. At the very center of the system the face of the despot "crystallizes all redundancies . . . emits and receives, releases and captures signifying signs" (TP 115). That face, in short, is the "substance of expression" that allows the whole system of "deterritorialized" signs to be "reterritorialized" in a circular feedback system constantly being recharged by the mediating interpreter–priests. Furthermore, be-cause a voice emanates from the face, what is written in the signifying regime always retains an "oral or non-book character": this would explain the essentially aural nature – the "crying" – of the imagery of Oedipa's heralded revelation. At the opposite ex-treme lies the face*less* figure of the scapegoat, always linked to the despot as a kind of "counterbody" with whom he communicates, but whose own body is tortured, humiliated, subjected to exile and exclusion. A potential threat at the periphery of the system, the scapegoat is always considered a point of disorder and noise:

> In the signifying regime, the scapegoat represents a new form of increasing entropy in the system of signs: it is charged with every-thing that was "bad" in a given period, that is, everything that resisted signifying signs, everything that eluded the referral from sign to sign through the different circles; it also assumes everything that was unable to recharge the signifier at its center and carries off everything that spills behind the outermost circle. Finally, and es-pecially, it incarnates the line of flight the signifying regime cannot tolerate, in other words, an absolute deterritorialization; the regime must block a line of this kind or define it in an entirely negative fashion precisely because it exceeds the degree of deterritorializa-tion of the signifying sign, however high it may be. (TP 116)

In other terms, the scapegoat functions both as the system's limit and as a point around which the signs that cannot be recharged and cycled back through the system by interpretation will gravi-tate. Eventually, these "negative" signs will accumulate until they must be discharged from the system along a "negative line of flight" in a ritual purification. However, with this "negative line of flight," the stage is set for a transformation into another regime of signs, the "post-signifying regime," which will come about through the reversal of the negative valence of the line of flight into a positive one. The result will be a mode of "subjectification" in which interpretation assumes a different functional value.

In *The Crying of Lot 49*, the Tristero assumes the structural posi-tion of the scapegoat. Pierce Inverarity, of course, occupies the position of the despot–god, which here simply means that he stands for the dominant and official cultural order. As we have already seen, the Tristero presents an inverse or negative image of this order: to manifest itself at all, it must assume a doubled or disguised form, masquerading its true otherness behind some apparent version of the official system. In short, its "signs" can appear only as distortions or disguises of the officially recognized signs; hence, in part of Inverarity's legacy – the postage stamp collection – the signs on the officially issued stamps of the U.S. Post Office are inverted or deformed in some way, thus "franking" (or disguising) Tristero under a government seal. At the same time, Tristero attracts and collects around itself the wayward signs that are unrecognizable to the official order, or those (like W.A.S.T.E) which are ambiguously positioned between the two orders: what is redundant for one is the primary mode of communication for the other. In relation to an official system, the Tristero represents the negative line of flight or escape. The interpreter–priests whom Oedipa encounters can neither verify its existence nor recharge the signifiers of the official and despotic order, which now only becomes more entropic as it is confused with the order of the scapegoat. However, for any transformation to occur, this negative line of flight will have to assume a positive valence. In this sense, again, *The Crying of Lot 49* is a transitional novel, perched ambiguously between dominant and preterite signifying orders. In the novel to follow, *Gravity's Rainbow,* the introduction of the "Counterforce" offers the possibility of a positive "line of flight." Is is no accident, then, that in *Gravity's Rainbow* paranoia assumes a positive valence, and functions as an order of subjectification or a means of producing new subjects.[12]

Some readers may feel that this process of reversal has already begun in *The Crying of Lot 49,* or at least is fully imminent: all that is needed is for Oedipa to make a "leap of faith," and the Tristero will really begin to exist. But such an act would require a different regime of signs, and our aim here has been to isolate the underlying structure or semiotic regime operating in the novel as a way of escaping its interpretive binds. Thus, while acknowledging that *The Crying of Lot 49* is a concrete and highly nuanced work of art, we must also see that it incarnates a *particular* regime of signs. Looking at it in these terms can release us from the limited third-person narrative perspective that "Oedipa Maas" mobilizes. Precisely because she is a character whose psychological coherence the narrative always maintains and supports, she can only conceptualize the relations between Pierce and Tristero as mutually exclusive and logically oppositional. As a *text*, however, *The Crying of Lot 49* must keep open a set of logically disjunctive possibilities, which means that it must behave as if they were all simultaneously true: all the interpreter–priests are "right" about the nature of the reality they interpret; Tristero is, at once, a practical joke, an historically verifiable conspiracy, and a figment of Oedipa's imagination; it is both the underground system that opposes the capitalistic one which Pierce's empire represents, and it structurally mimes the dominant order. In this sense, Pynchon's novel is a schizo-text, and presents a disjunctive synthesis of diverse and incompatible views. It can do this, finally, because of its underlying coherence as a specific regime of signs, or a structure not dependent upon any particular point of view, but on the endless proliferation of signs calling for endlessly repeatable acts of interpretation.

NOTES

1. I take the phrase "regime of signs" from the chapter "587 B.C.–A.D. 70: On Several Regimes of Signs," in Gilles Deleuze and Félix Guattari, *A Thousand Plateaus: Capitalism and Schizophrenia*, trans. Brian Massumi (Minneapolis: University of Minnesota Press, 1987), pp. 111–48. (Subsequent references will be to this edition and will be noted parenthetically in the text with the abbreviation TP.) Deleuze and Guattari call "any specific expression a regime of signs, at least when the expression is linguistic" (TP 111). They immediately add that "a regime of signs constitutes a semiotic system," but that semiotic systems are difficult to analyze in themselves. Nevertheless, the authors begin with a particular regime of signs, the "signifying" or "semiotic" regime, which privileges the formal process of signification. Later, however, they show that there is no formalized, autonomous linguistic system that operates independently of all forms of content. They argue therefore for a fully pragmatic, anti-universalist approach to language. As I hope to show, the entire chapter throws a great deal of light on the "semiotic regime" at work in *The Crying of Lot 49*.

2. Quoted in Deleuze and Guattari, *A Thousand Plateaus*, p. 112. See Claude Lévi-Strauss, "Introduction à l'oeuvre de Marcel Mauss," in Marcel Mauss, *Sociologie et anthropologie* (Paris: PUF, 1973), pp. 48–9. Lévi-Strauss emphasizes the peculiarity that at the outset of the pro-

cess of signification, the "signified" is given without being known. Only gradually will it be revealed, whereas the system of signifiers is complete all at once. As we will see, this "inadequation" between the two orders is crucial for the signifying or semiotic regime.

3. In a rigorous semiotic sense, of course, Pynchon's novel is not only composed of signs but full of them. In order to avoid possible confusion and a cumbersome technical nomenclature, I shall use the term "sign" almost exclusively in reference to Oedipa's special or "sensitized" experience. My use of the word will thus correspond to something like "sign" taken in the more archaic sense of "omen" or "portent." In strictly semiotic terms, it is a secondary sign in a staggered or connotative system. For a discussion of such a system, see Roland Barthes, *Elements of Semiology* (1964; rpt. New York: Noonday Press, 1988), pp. 89–94.

4. For a discussion of these two patterns, see Anne Mangel, "Maxwell's Demon, Entropy, Information: *The Crying of Lot 49*," and W. T. Lhamon, Jr., "Pentecost, Promiscuity and Pynchon's *V.*," in *Mindful Pleasures: Essays on Thomas Pynchon*, ed. George Levine and David Leverenz (Boston: Little, Brown, 1976), pp. 87–100, 69–86. See also James Norhnberg, "Pynchon's Paraclete," and Edward Mendelson, "The Sacred, the Profane, and *The Crying of Lot 49*," in *Pynchon: A Collection of Critical Essays*, ed. Edward Mendelson (Englewood Cliffs, N.J.: Prentice-Hall, 1978), pp. 147–61, 112–46.

5. This motif is registered in a variety of contexts – for example, in Oedipa's exchange with Genghis Cohen, when he notes that in spring the dandelion wine gets cloudy, as if this were a sign that the wine remembered its former existence as flowers (cf. pp. 98–9), and most poignantly in Oedipa's exchange with the dying sailor, with whose death untold collections of information will be lost. However, the sailor will persist in Oedipa's memory as the bearer of the Tristero sign and in the letter he writes to his wife. About this persistence of the sign, Deleuze and Guattari note:

Whether it passes into other signs or is kept in reserve for a time, the sign survives both its state of things and its signified; it leaps like an animal or dead person to regain its place in the chain and invest a new state, a new signified, from which it will in turn extricate itself. A hint of the eternal return. There is a whole regime of roving, floating statements, suspended names, signs lying in wait to return and be propelled by the chain. The signifier is the self-redundancy of the deterritorialized sign, a funereal world of terror. (TP 113)

As we will see, interpretation is what maintains this "eternal return" of the sign.

6. Although *The Crying of Lot 49* bears some resemblance to James's own

structurally ambiguous story, "The Turn of the Screw," there is this crucial difference: in James's story the ambiguity concerning the governess's experience exists only for the reader, whereas in Pynchon's novel the multiple possibilities are internalized in Oedipa's consciousness. If James's story turns on an unresolvable ambiguity and articulates a truly either/or structural logic, Pynchon's novel is a "schizo-text" that maintains the potential validity of possibilities which remain mutually exclusive for both Oedipa and the reader. For this reason, moreover, there can be no language adequate to its "multiversal" vision. For a discussion of the contemporary novel as "schizo-text," see Allen Thiher, *Words in Reflection: Modern Language Theory and Postmodern Fiction* (Chicago: University of Chicago Press, 1984), especially pp. 131–55.

7. The title of the story published in *Esquire* (December 1965) is "The World (This One), the Flesh (Mrs. Oedipa Maas) and the Testament of Pierce Inverarity."

8. Mendelson, "The Sacred, the Profane, and *The Crying of Lot 49*," p.123.

9. We should perhaps acknowledge here that it would be neither anachronistic nor inappropriate to stress the gender difference of Oedipa's position vis-à-vis the male interpreters. In this sense, our efforts to uncover and reveal the novel's semiotic structure could also be used to support a feminist or proto-feminist reading.

10. Both Mendelson and Lhamon, in the essays cited above, make a similar point, but each with a different emphasis. For Mendelson, the Pentecostal imagery associated with the Tristero heralds a truly religious revelation for Oedipa (its "content"), whereas for Lhamon it designates the inception or "inspiriting" of "toungued speech" – a mixed, anti-edifying and anti-formal mode of discourse – into the modern world. A semiotic approach, however, would want to distinguish here between forms of content and forms of expression. In part IV, I approach the novel in terms of the latter, specifically as a signifying regime of signs which can accommodate a variety of mixed forms of content – religious, historical, psychological – without privileging or inflecting interpretation exclusively toward any one.

11. See Deleuze and Guattari, *A Thousand Plateaus*, pp. 111–48. The four regimes of signs are: the semiotic or signifying, the presignifying, the countersignifying, and the post-signifying.

12. See my essay "Pynchon's Zone: A Postmodern Multiplicity," *Arizona Quarterly* 46, no. 3 (Autumn 1990): 91–122.

4

"Hushing Sick Transmissions": Disrupting Story in *The Crying of Lot 49*

BERNARD DUYFHUIZEN

"THE sight of sawdust, even pencil shavings, made [Mucho Maas] wince, his own kind being known to use it for hushing sick transmissions" (13). Although this image of consumerist deception appears on its face simply to be a symptom of Mucho's inability "to believe in" the used car lot where he once worked, it uncovers for us a matrix of *transmissions* beyond the doctored gear boxes of beat-up Chevrolets. In automobiles, a transmission is the linkage necessary for transferring power into positive motion. If the gear box has been "doctored" (paradoxical jargon for "contaminated") with sawdust, it cannot communicate its decay on the way to breakdown — the sawdust disrupts both communication, and ultimately, the transfer of power. Such a deception seems to define an America out of touch with its "founding" commercial values of integrity and truth-in-lending, and it hints at a key element of inquiry Thomas Pynchon pursues in *The Crying of Lot 49*: How does a culture or society transmit a heritage — its ideals or its corruptions — and how are these transmissions disrupted?

This fundamental question, however, suggests further questions that Pynchon wants his readers to ask: What *are* our cultural transmissions? How are cultural patterns valorized by a society formed from precursor social structures? How are these patterns produced to meet local needs for order and control? How do they establish a status quo that strives always to reproduce itself and, thus, to ensure the unencumbered transmission of sociocultural formations to the next generation? When asking these questions we must remember that cultural and social formation always implies the construction of a social hierarchy, complete with myths of power and privilege. Hence, we must ask whether the systems of cultural formation that operate within a given society paradox-ically represent both something to be maintained and a process of positive motion toward an "improved" cultural formation (the myth of Utopia), or whether these systems become the sawdust that masks the decay of a society (the myth of dystopia) – a disruption that makes us deaf to the "truth" about the world in which we live.

Since cultural formation occurs in the incessant textualization of privileged representations, Pynchon in *The Crying of Lot 49* asks his readers to look for texts beyond those sanctioned and visible, to listen for the sounds of "silence." He brings the image of silence to the textual surface when Oedipa Maas, exhausted from her twenty-four-hour odyssey through San Francisco, returns to her hotel, finds a lobby full of delegates to a deaf-mute convention, and is swept up by a crowd heading for the grand ballroom:

> She tried to struggle out of the silent, gesturing swarm, but was too weak. Her legs ached, her mouth tasted horrible. They swept her on into the ballroom, where she was seized about the waist by a hand-some young man in a Harris tweed coat and waltzed round and round, through the rustling, shuffling hush, under a great unlit chandelier. Each couple on the floor danced whatever was in the fellow's head: tango, two-step, bossa nova, slop. But how long, Oedipa thought, could it go on before collisions became a serious hindrance? There would have to be collisions. The only alternative was some unthinkable order of music, many rhythms, all keys at once, a choreography in which each couple meshed easy, pre-destined. Something they all heard with an extra sense atrophied in herself. She followed her partner's lead, limp in the young mute's clasp, waiting for the collisions to begin. But none came. (131)

Oedipa, a parodic everywoman of 1960s middle-class America, finds in this silent ballroom full of dancing couples a cultural for-mation to which she is alien – a system of communal order inside a seeming anarchy that occurs beyond her particular patterns of logic; the necessary collisions never occur. Additionally, this scene is emblematic of the paradox Oedipa herself becomes during the course of the text, an everywoman whose journey to the center of things is also a journey to the margins of possibility and to her own crisis of what "to believe in." To see how she arrives at this dual position, we must view Oedipa as the figure of transmission, the channel that will mediate the matrix of cultural information and memory that by conventional paradigms should be flowing from its source to its destination. We come to discover, however, that neither source nor destination are finite and that the messages transmitted refuse to resolve into a single meaning; instead, the messages disseminate fragments of meaning across a culture that has lost any totalizing mythology. As Anne Mangel has observed, "[t]he pursuit of meaning in language turns into a chimera throughout the novel as information constantly disintegrates through transmission."[1]

Meaning, in *The Crying of Lot 49*, is never simple. From the very outset, when Oedipa discovers that she has to execute Pierce Inverarity's will, questions proliferate faster than answers. Yet, as culturally inscribed in the history of the novel as a literary genre, a will is supposed to complete the text of one's life: it is the epilogue to a life story. As Walter Benjamin writes in "The Storyteller": "Death is the sanction of everything that the storyteller can tell."[2] The completed life becomes both narratable and transmissible – the will serving as a textual link that inscribes as textuality that which is inherited. But what worked for countless nineteenth-century novels no longer produces the same kind of satisfying textuality in the postmodern world of *The Crying of Lot 49*. Wills signify in legal discursive systems the orderly transfer of property, the collected semiotic material that frames (and in an increasingly materialistic culture, defines) the individual existence. Yet now this transfer of property is often anything but "orderly" as relatives struggle over objects, asserting their rights to give meaning to collected material. Within this context, Inverarity's will represents a dislocation of codes: there are no squabbling relatives – there is only Oedipa – and there appears to be no limit to his estate, as Oedipa, near the end of the novel, comes to realize:

> She walked down a stretch of railroad track next to the highway. Spurs ran off here and there into factory property. Pierce may have owned these factories too. But did it matter now if he'd owned all of San Narciso? San Narciso was a name; an incident among our climatic records of dreams and what dreams became among our accumulated daylight, a moment's squall-line or tornado's touch-down among the higher, more continental solemnities – storm-

systems of group suffering and need, prevailing winds of affluence. There was the true continuity, San Narciso had no boundaries. No one knew yet how to draw them. She had dedicated herself, weeks ago, to making sense of what Inverarity had left behind, never suspecting that the legacy was America. (177–8)

But what kind of legacy is this? "Might Oedipa Maas yet be his heiress?" And if so (the novel is provocatively ambiguous here), what does she really inherit – his assets? San Narciso? America? At each remove the orderly transfer becomes more fantastic, yet for a man whose name may be a portmanteau derived from the philatic term "inverse rarity," shouldn't we expect an inverse logic from his last testament, an inverse system of transmission for his "property"?[3] Oedipa comes to wonder whether Inverarity "might have written the testament only to harass a one-time mistress. . . . Or he might even have tried to survive death, as a paranoia; as a pure conspiracy against someone he loved" (178–9). Either way, Inverarity may represent the attempt of the individual subject to project precisely what Benjamin suggests becomes transmissible to the storyteller at the moment of death: "authority" over the representation of one's life. As Benjamin avers, "[t]his authority is at the very source of the story."[4]

Applying a transmission theory of narrative to this exchange leads us to question the status of "authority."[5] As its etymology demonstrates, authority derives from "author," the originator, inventory, source of a text. The "text," in the present case of Pierce Inverarity, is the literal will, which is both a metaphor for his life story and a metonym for Oedipa's life story. In this complex relationship, Oedipa must try to make sense of things by becoming a storyteller. Yet how does one become a storyteller in what Jean Baudrillard calls the "hyperreality" of contemporary culture, a culture saturated with media and messages that are simulations of inherently displaced objects that no longer can be explained in a code based on any logocentric paradigm of referentiality?[6] Indeed, how can Oedipa hope to transform her authority, assigned for whatever reason by the subject of her story, into an "authoritative" tale that will satisfy both herself and the laws of probate? She feels that "[i]f it was really Pierce's attempt to leave an organized something behind after his own annihilation, then it was part of her duty, wasn't it, to bestow life on what had persisted . . . to bring the estate into pulsing stelliferous Meaning" (81–2). Yet by the end of Chapter 4, Oedipa begins to wonder "whether, at the end of this (if it were supposed to end), she too might not be left with only compiled memories of clues, announcements, intimations, but never the central truth itself, which must somehow each time be too bright for her memory to hold; which must always blaze out, destroying its own message irreversibly, leaving an overexposed blank when the ordinary world came back" (95).

This image of total transmission breakdown haunts Oedipa – to achieve insight beyond the ordinary is to test the parameters of belief in the actuality of a "central truth." Indeed, in Chapter 5, as Oedipa sets out from the Greek Way to begin her drift through a San Francisco night, she realizes her dilemma: "Each clue that comes is *supposed* to have its own clarity, its fine chances for permanence. But then she wondered if the gemlike 'clues' were only some kind of compensation. To make up for her having lost the direct, epileptic Word, the cry that might abolish the night" (118). Not only does this passage signal that each hint of a center is also a confirmation of the margin, but it violates the organizing principles of English grammar. The third "sentence" only makes sense in apposition to the second; thus, in its syntax it underscores the essential separation of "gemlike 'clues' " from the "direct, epileptic Word." This separation marks the failure of Oedipa to mediate completely the different transmissions occurring in the fictional culture of *The Crying of Lot 49.*

As at other similar moments in the novel, such as her first glimpse of San Narciso, Oedipa senses she is on the brink of a "revelation [that trembles] just past the threshold of her understanding" (24). Although the conventional teleology of a story is to arrive at a still point of "understanding," Oedipa increasingly fears that she will be unsatisfied with the outcome of her quest to know the "central truth" of Inverarity's will. This quest to know is also the desire of the storyteller for an authoritative tale. Oedipa's quest in *The Crying of Lot 49* is to become the storyteller, yet to fulfill that quest she must seek a coherent story amid the myriad pieces of information and conflicted transmissions she discovers. This conflicted matrix of transmissions marks, as well, a cultural shift from the oral narrative tradition of the storyteller Benjamin discusses, to the multimedia simulations Baudrillard exposes in contemporary culture and in the very conception of America itself – Oedipa's legacy.

In "The Storyteller," Benjamin assets that "the art of storytelling is coming to an end. Less and less frequently do we encounter people with the ability to tell a tale properly. More and more often there is embarrassment all around when the wish to hear a story is expressed. It is as if something that seemed inalienable to us, the securest among our possessions, were taken from us: the ability to exchange experiences."[7] Significantly for Benjamin's argument, the exchange of experience requires the oral storyteller whose tale embodies the cultural memory of events and people. In opposition to the storyteller, Benjamin cites the purveyors of "information" who reduce events to facts and processed explanations: "The value of information does not survive the moment in which it was new. It lives only at that moment; it has to surrender to it completely and explain itself to it without losing any time. A story is different. It does not expend itself. It preserves and concentrates its strength and is capable of releasing it even after a long time."[8]

In many respects, Oedipa Maas is the figure of this dichotomy between story and information. Her first name parodically echoes a foundation story in Western culture: Oedipus, whose story, as told by Sophocles, is an amalgam of storytelling exchanges, the enforced repetition of cultural memories perhaps repressed but never forgotten. Yet her last name, Maas, also implies "mass," which in turn implies the mass communication networks of the present era. If told on the six o'clock news, would information about Oedipus's actions merely shock us rather than move us to catharsis, to a recognition of our flawed nature? Oedipa's attempt to construct a story through various moments of oral exchange is disrupted by the hints of Tristero that surface in every story she encounters; and as these hints accumulate, Oedipa realizes the impossibility of exchanging experiences in the modern world. Tristero, the secret mail courier system that comes to obsess Oedipa and to deflect her from her original task of executing the will (though she comes to wonder whether they aren't connected after all), is a counternarrative to the one articulated by official power and embodied in the national postal system. As an underground system, Tristero offers the possibility of epistolary stories, though in reality the messages sent by WASTE turn out to be as much waste as the junk mail delivered by the official carriers. Nevertheless, Oedipa's awareness of this counterstory's existence leads her to pursue it, to try to become its storyteller even though her sources exchange their tales with, at best, a "ritual reluctance" (79).

Two scenes of oral exchange in *The Crying of Lot 49* exemplify Oedipa's attempt to recapture memory via the transmission of story. The first is her interview with Mr. Thoth, whom she seemingly randomly discovers because of her "what you might have to call, growing obsession, with 'bringing something of herself' – even if that something was just her presence – to the scatter of business interests that had survived Inverarity. She would give them order, she would create constellations" (90) or, as she calls it earlier in the novel, "stelliferous Meaning." By trying to bring something of herself to the story she wants to construct, Oedipa tries to fulfill Benjamin's stricture to inject what she discovers into her life as a storyteller so that she will be able to express it again – "traces of the storyteller cling to the story."[9] In encountering Mr. Thoth, Oedipa comes face to face with an embodiment of the storytelling of another era. As he wakes from dozing in front of the television, Mr. Thoth immediately engages the convention of storytelling transmission as he foregrounds his mediating position:

> "I was dreaming," Mr. Thoth told her, "about my grandfather. A very old man, at least as old as I am now, 91. I thought, when I was a boy, that he had been 91 all his life. Now I feel," laughing, "as if *I* have been 91 all my life. Oh, the stories that old man would tell. He rode for the Pony Express, back in the gold rush days. His horse was named Adolf, I remember that." (91)[10]

Mr. Thoth goes on to tell Oedipa that his grandfather was an Indian killer, but more importantly, that he once had an encounter with the "Indians who weren't Indians." Although brief, this story, with its corroborating talisman of the ring he shows her, rehearses for Oedipa the same plot elements she had heard in the account of the GIs killed at Lago de Pietà and in *The Courier's Tragedy* (and that she will later uncover in *The Singular Peregrinations of Dr. Diocletian Blobb*).

The repetition of identical plot elements in stories placed in widely divergent contexts sets up an uncanny sense of coincidence, yet in *The Crying of Lot 49* the fine line between randomness and pattern is always under question. The text complicates our sense of this line by its transmission procedures. Through much of the novel Oedipa receives her stories second- and third-hand, always displaced from the originary moment. Moreover, these stories disrupt themselves: Manny Di Presso's account of American GI bones used for cigarette filters is open to question because its source is an organized crime figure; *The Courier's Tragedy* becomes a problem of textual transmission as Oedipa tries to account for the line mentioning Trystero in the performance she has witnessed; and Mr. Thoth himself is barely able to keep his memories of his grandfather separated from the cartoons he watches on television. Oedipa needs to experience Tristero firsthand if she is every going to make sense of this strange detour in her quest for the authoritative tale of Inverarity.

Oedipa's odyssey through San Francisco in Chapter 5 brings her closer to a sense of Tristero's reality at the same time that she comes to realize how marginally she is positioned in relation to that reality. To become the storyteller, Oedipa must try to move from the margin to the center, and her opportunity comes when "[t]hrough an open doorway, on the stair leading up into the disinfectant-smelling twilight of a rooming house she saw an old man huddled, shaking with grief she couldn't hear" (125). Like another Greek hero, Odysseus, Oedipa enters this symbolic realm of the dead to bring back a message from the enactment of self-discovery. Benjamin asserts that one of the archaic representatives of the storyteller is "the trading seaman," the carrier of "the lore of faraway places."[11] Odysseus of course fills this role in the *Odyssey*, but by the time Western culture has reached Pynchon's vision of San Francisco in *The Crying of Lot 49*, Odysseus has become the decrepit sailor Oedipa encounters on the rooming-house steps, a seaman who will never make it home to his wife in Fresno and who asks Oedipa to post "a letter that looked like he'd been carrying it around for years" (125).

On one level, the sailor's story has lost its oral dimension, reduced to a text that may never reach his Penelope, whose patience, by now, has probably worn quite thin. Yet on another level, as Oedipa looks at him she perceives a different encryption of his tale — a tale that would someday

> end among the flaming, secret salts held all those years by the insatiable stuffing of a mattress that could keep vestiges of every nightmare seat, helpless overflowing bladder, viciously, tearfully consummated wet dream, like the memory bank to a computer of the lost[.] She was overcome all at once by a need to touch him, as if she could not believe in him, or would not remember him without it. (126)

This transmission and exchange through human contact is one of the most moving scenes in all of Pynchon's writing.[12] Yet, as the scene develops, Oedipa is increasingly drawn to the insight that at this moment, when the sailor's letter has given her the key to the empirical existence of Tristero, it is the metaphoric formation of existence that dominates perception: "The act of metaphor then was a thrust at truth and a lie, depending where you were: inside, safe, or outside, lost. Oedipa did not know where she was" (129).

Oedipa's uncertainty is figured in the play on DT/dt (delirium tremens/time differential). In the high magic of low puns, Oedipa recognizes that "DT's must give access to dt's of spectra beyond the known sun, music made purely of Antarctic loneliness and fright" (129). Again, as with the deaf-mute dancing that soon follows this moment in the narrative, Oedipa experiences something beyond the visible realm of her limited, culturally inscribed perceptions. This glimmering hint, however, is nothing more than that — Oedipa recognizes her helplessness to preserve either the story the sailor has to transmit or the sailor himself. Although Oedipa will follow the trail of an apparent Tristero courier, this experience does not become "story," it becomes "data" that Oedipa knows she has verified, yet "she wanted it all to be fantasy" (132).

After the experience with the sailor, Oedipa's actions become increasingly mechanical and distant. Her contact with those who have surrounded her quest begins to unravel — Hilarius flips out, Mucho trips out, Metzger runs off, Driblette checks out, Zapf's Used Books burns down, and so on — until she makes her last stand at the novel's closing auction. The process of disruption and loss that leads Oedipa to all but total isolation signifies the entropy of

Oedipa's life story, where gains in the quantity of information are offset by the gradual destruction of the story itself. Nevertheless, it would be reductive to say that only one moment in the text stages this shift from story to information; indeed, Oedipa still desires the authoritative story even at the end, but there seems to be a conspiracy against her. Ultimately, Oedipa comes to embody the postmodern condition of information overload – like a reader of postmodern fiction (Pynchon's own novels, for example), Oedipa cannot keep all of the fragments together in one totalized story. As Molly Hite has observed, the "absent insight" that will lead to the "Holy Center" of Pynchon's fictional universe is always displaced and deferred.[13]

But displacement and deferral pervade Pynchon's novel from its very first sentences, which are watched over by the "greenish dead eye of the TV tube" (9). Television, video, and filmmaking are to become significant foci in *Vineland*,[14] and in *The Crying of Lot 49* we can see an early example of Pynchon's fascination with television and the creation of television culture.[15] This fictional deployment of television has already been noted in Mr. Thoth's cartoon-altered consciousness, and it plays a side role in Oedipa's encounter with John Nefastis, but it is most apparent in the novel's second chapter, when Oedipa and her co-executor, the lawyer Metzger, first meet to discuss Inverarity's will (28–43). At first she cannot believe in his reality:

> He turned out to be so good-looking that Oedipa thought at first They, somebody up there, were putting her on. It had to be an actor. He stood at the door, behind him the oblong pool shimmering silent in a mild diffusion of light from the nighttime sky, saying, "Mrs. Maas," like a reproach. His enormous eyes, lambent, extravagantly lashed, smiled out at her wickedly; she looked around him for reflectors, microphones, camera cabling, but there was only himself and a debonair bottle of French Beaujolais, which he claimed to've smuggled last year into California, this rollicking lawbreaker, past the frontier guards. (28)

In the passage, the dialogic intersection of discourses is striking. At first, Oedipa can only organize Metzger through her still-budding paranoia as a simulation – not a real lawyer but an actor playing a part. Oedipa's regular lawyer, Roseman, with his obsessive views on the "Perry Mason" television series (18–20), has foregrounded this reading, and as the plot of the novel develops Oedipa will increasingly wonder whether everything she has experienced has been staged. Oedipa's simulated reading of Metzger as actor is intensified by the double framing of the door and the pool that focuses him against the night sky backdrop. The description of his first words and of his eyes then slips into the voice of Raymond Chandler, and if we associate this description with Oedipa's point of view, is it any wonder that she starts looking for the camera? Even when it is "only himself" and a bottle of wine, the indirect telling of the *story* of the wine echoes certain movie plot cliches, which Pynchon's narrator undercuts in the voice of a studio promoter hyping a situation comedy starring "this rollicking lawbreaker."

By destabilizing this "cute meet," Pynchon wants to question the status of the "real." As Jean Baudrillard writes, "Reality itself founders in hyperrealism, the meticulous reduplication of the real, preferably through another reproductive medium, such as photography."[16] We can safety extend Baudrillard's example to include film and television; indeed, the cultural function of both has been the massive production and reproduction of images that within contemporary culture underscores Oscar Wilde's adage: "Life imitates Art." Yet Pynchon's substitutions are never simple metaphors: Metzger looks like an actor; then we discover a few sentences later that he actually once was a child actor, driven by a stagestruck mother, and "'You know what mothers like that turn their male children into'" (29). Metzger deploys a Freudian reading (yet another metaphor) to rationalize his oedipal upbringing, to which Oedipa replies, "'You certainly don't look,'" only to be cut short by her own counter-rationalization of the apparent discontinuity of images, perhaps recognizing that at the level of signs her own name reproduces a medium for telling his story. In Metzger, we see a startling contrast between Benjamin's conception of "story" and the hyperreality of California culture, in which the carefully constructed *look* is projected and reproduced in a symbolic exchange of signs or "realities" that are always simulations of simulations. Metzger may argue that "Looks don't mean a thing any more. . . . I live inside by looks, and I'm never sure" (29), but we know better.

Yet Oedipa may prefer hyperreality to story: when Metzger suggests that he and Inverarity had once discussed her, she snaps on the TV to avoid hearing about herself. What blooms onto the screen is the movie *Cashiered,* starring none other than Baby Igor – Metzger the child actor. From here the coincidences proliferate; not only with Metzger in the film, but the commercials that frame the segments of the film all promote Inverarity interests: Fangoso Lagoons (the map of which reminds Oedipa of her earlier hierophanic moment where she compared San Narciso to a giant printed circuit – one of the novel's many technological metaphors for the means of transmission and reproduction), Beaconsfield Cigarettes, and Hogan's Seraglio. The corporate holdings, the assets to be transmitted to Inverarity's heirs, are now reproduced in broadcast images that trade only in the production of desire, yet we might question whether that desire is for a real product or merely for a simulation captured in the semiotics of advertising. This matrix of simulations comes to overwhelm Oedipa to the point that she cannot disengage her life from the incessant reduplication of images.

Again, Metzger serves to represent this matrix of reproduction. At one point, Metzger tells Oedipa that he had recontextualized as a tax write-off her fondly remembered trip with Inverarity to Mexico. This revaluing of her cherished experience prompts Oedipa to accuse Metzger of being, along with Perry Mason, a shyster, to which he responds with an explication of the connection between lawyers and actors:

> "But our beauty lies," explained Metzger, "in this extended capacity for convolution. A lawyer in a courtroom, in front of a jury, becomes an actor, right? Raymond Burr is an actor impersonating a lawyer, who in front of a jury becomes an actor. Me, I'm a former actor who became a lawyer. They've done a pilot film of a TV series, in fact, based loosely on my career, starring my friend Manny Di Presso, a one-time lawyer who quit his firm to become an actor. Who in this pilot plays me, an actor become a lawyer reverting periodically to being an actor. The film is in an air-conditioned vault

at one of the Hollywood studios, light can't fatigue it, it can be repeated endlessly." (33)

Yet most pilot TV shows are never broadcast in the first place, so the endless repetition (and it probably *can't* be repeated while it is safe in that vault) marks an already emptied means of reproduction. Moreover, it should not surprise us that Di Presso shows up in the next chapter at Fangoso Lagoons, once again a lawyer, now building a case against the Inverarity estate over the bones used in the Beaconsfield cigarette project. That this has filiations with Mr. Thoth and *The Courier's Tragedy,* as well as to other clues Oedipa traces, suggests the hyperreal intertextuality that is woven through the various transmissions of the text. The lines of demarcation between transmissions disappear, hushed in a way that disrupts any hope Oedipa (or the reader) might have for the emergence of a univocal "story."

At this point, Pynchon teaches us how to read *The Crying of Lot 49.* The plot of Metzger's evening with Oedipa becomes entangled with the plot of the film *Cashiered.* To fulfill his desired tryst with Oedipa, Metzger engages in a game dynamic based on determining the plot and ending of the film. The plot of the game entails their sexual liaison, which ultimately, as it turns out, follows the archetypal plot of sexual conquest in a paradoxical relation to the plot of military failure depicted in the film. This intersection of plots, however, is not simply an alternation we might structurally chart; instead, the film reels are shown out of order, disrupting the continuity of Oedipa's reading in such a way as to call into question the teleological convention she expresses: "'All those movies have happy endings.'" Since Metzger will not give her odds, Oedipa hedges her bet (that the film will not end with the conventional happy ending) and disrupts the game – Strip Botticelli – by donning nearly every piece of clothing she has available. In the humor of this parody of epic preparation, capped by the flight of the hair spray can, we can see again the influence of television culture as Oedipa's acts of avoidance rival any that Lucille Ball concocted during the years of "I Love Lucy."

Nevertheless, there is an underside to this scene: as Oedipa seeks to build her defenses by overdressing, she deconstructs the erotics of the fashion system and the semiotics of the scantily clad image on the sign of the Echo Courts Motel. Clothes confer power and control within social contexts; but like the spray can that starts careening around the bathroom after she knocks it over, Oedipa's power is limited and will be exhausted by Metzger's persistence. In the process, Oedipa loses a sense of her identity; the intrusion of Metzger into her life disrupts the transmission of her life story as faithful housewife. The condition she enters unknowingly is that of becoming – a process of shifting states of being that shakes her out of her Young Republican complacency and toward a more radical formation of her self.

Added to this already full scene is the performance of the Paranoids, a musical simulation of 1960s British rock'n'roll. Not only does their music drown out Oedipa and Metzger's conversation (which is already disrupted and incomplete), but it comes to coincide with the intersection of transmissions that are about to climax around Oedipa. The game of Strip Botticelli mutates into Metzger's playing with Oedipa as if she were a "Barbie doll," removing the layers of clothing: "She may have fallen asleep once or twice. She awoke at last to find herself getting laid; she'd come in on a sexual crescendo in progress, like a cut to a scene where the camera's already moving. Outside the fugue of guitars had begun" (42). Oedipa has become nearly totally passive as the metaphors suggest the intersection of music and the cinematic. Orgasm, however, coincides with a power blackout: "Her climax and Metzger's, when it came, coincided with every light in the place, including the TV tube, suddenly going out, dead, black" (42). The power's return coincides with the movie's ending – the tragic ending Oedipa had predicted. Although she has "won" the game, she loses in the end. Metzger has exploited Oedipa's weakness for storytelling by engaging her in a game that trades only in information, in hyperreal fragments that defy conventional reconstruction. By this means he achieves her submission, and, as we have come to recognize in the novel, Oedipa's actions are always haunted by paradigms of submission to forces beyond her control, forces perhaps set up by Inverarity, forces that always reorder the plot away from a teleology that will resolve itself into order.

Oedipa's submissions to the transmissive power of other cultural

92

formations present a difficulty for readers who desire her success in the quest, and who also desire success in their own teleologies of reading. Pynchon perhaps saw Oedipa as kin to Herbert Stencil in *V.* and Tyrone Slothrop in *Gravity's Rainbow* – seekers of coherent stories who end up clutching fragments of information rather than a unified truth. In *Vineland,* Pynchon writes of a stronger group of women, especially DL Chastain, whose battle with power, embodied in Brock Vond, does not presuppose her submission. The women in that novel take over the technology of hyperreality – the film cameras and videotapes – to record their stories and provide a record of the abuses of power. But Oedipa works increasingly alone, trapped in solipsistic transmissions that self-disrupt in moments of extreme doubt. The set of signs that comes together for Oedipa cannot be exchanged in the medium of "story" because variability and indeterminacy have replaced the older models of narrative transmission that once served to order our world.

Can Oedipa tell her "story" to anyone, can it find a form for its telling? Rather than a story of inheritance, is it ultimately the story of disinheritance, a story of the disenfranchisement of Oedipa Maas? At the close of the introduction to *Slow Learner,* Pynchon seems to disinherit *The Crying of Lot 49* when he comments somewhat disparagingly that this "story . . . was marketed as a 'novel.' "[17] As readers, we consume "novels" in particular ways based on the codes and conventions of reading that we bring to a text. Pynchon has always challenged our habitual conventions of reading, asking us to trace other possibilities within the variable codes of his writing. We end the text with "Oedipa settled back, to await the crying of lot 49" (183); if the truth is to come, it comes in the void, the hushed silence of the blank end pages – the pages upon which many readers begin to inscribe their own texts of interpretation. In *Vineland,* Pynchon briefly visits the fictional universe of *The Crying of Lot 49,* but all we discover is that Mucho Maas "decided around 1967, after a divorce remarkable even in that more innocent time for its geniality, to go into record producing."[18] Although hardly the continuation we may desire, at least we can infer that Oedipa got out of the auction room. Small comfort.

NOTES

1. Anne Mangel, "Maxwell's Demon, Entropy, Information: *The Crying of Lot 49*," in *Mindful Pleasures: Essays on Thomas Pynchon*, ed. George Levine and David Leverenz (Boston: Little, Brown, 1976), p. 96.
2. Walter Benjamin, "The Storyteller: Reflections of the Works of Nikolai Leskov," in *Illuminations*, trans. Harry Zohn (New York: Harcourt, Brace & World, 1968), p. 94.
3. Richard Poirier makes this point in his essay "The Importance of Thomas Pynchon," in *Mindful Pleasures*, p. 22.
4. Benjamin, "The Storyteller," p. 94.
5. For more on transmission theory, see my "Mimesis, Authority, and Belief in Narrative Poetics: Toward a Transmission Theory for a Poetics of Fiction," *Novel* 18 (1985): 217–22; more specifically on the topic of authority, see Ralph Flores, *The Rhetoric of Doubtful Authority: Deconstructive Readings of Self-Questioning Narratives, St. Augustine to Faulkner* (Ithaca: Cornell University Press, 1984), and my "Questions of Authority and (Dis)Belief in Literary Theory," *New Orleans Review* 12, 3 (1985): 67–74.
6. See Jean Baudrillard, "Symbolic Exchange and Death" and "Simulacra and Simulations," in *Jean Baudrillard: Selected Writings*, ed. Mark Poster (Stanford: Stanford University Press, 1988), pp. 119–48, 166–84.
7. Benjamin, "The Storyteller," p. 83.
8. Ibid., p. 90.
9. Ibid., p. 92.
10. Uncannily, Benjamin writes a passage that echoes Mr. Thoth's meditation on age and remembrance: "A man – so says the truth that was meant here – who died at thirty-five will appear to *remembrance* at every point in his life as a man who dies at the age of thirty-five. In other words, the statement that makes no sense for real life becomes indisputable for remembered life." (Ibid., p. 100)
11. Ibid., pp. 84–5.
12. Compare Oedipa's gesture to help the sailor with a scene such as Franz Pökler's trying to comfort a concentration camp survivor in *Gravity's Rainbow* (New York: Viking, 1973), pp. 432–3.
13. Molly Hite, *Ideas of Order in the Novels of Thomas Pynchon* (Columbus: Ohio State University Press, 1983).
14. As early as *V.* (Philadelphia: Lippincott, 1963), Pynchon creates Fergus Mixolydian, who, by implanting a switch "on the inner skin of his forearm[,] . . . became an extension of the TV set" (p. 56).

Vineland (Boston: Little, Brown, 1990) presents us with representations of 1980s California, where television has saturated the culture to the point that one character – Hector Zuñiga, a true "Tubefreak" – has to be taken to a "Tubaldetox" center.

15. An excellent source for understanding the cultural aspects of television is John Fiske, *Television Culture* (London: Methuen, 1987).
16. Baudrillard, "Symbolic Exchange and Death," p. 144.
17. Thomas Pynchon, *Slow Learner: Early Stories* (Boston: Little, Brown, 1984), p. 22.
18. *Vineland,* p. 309.

5

"A Metaphor of God Knew How Many Parts": The Engine that Drives *The Crying of Lot 49*

N. KATHERINE HAYLES

NEARLY everyone who has written about *The Crying of Lot 49* has commented on the ambiguous ending. A sense of mystery or irresolution hangs over the novel even after one has read and reread it many times. Many readers take the lingering ambiguities to signal that *The Crying of Lot 49* is a postmodern text, more interested in revealing the constructed nature of consensual reality than in mimetically reflecting a world that exists independent of our perceptions.[1] Yet as the novel draws to a close there is also a growing sense of limitation, as if Oedipa were coming up against irreducible constraints that limit interpretation and circumscribe action.[2] It may be, then, that the underlying ambiguity of the novel rests between a postmodern view that renders irrelevant the distinctions between life and art, and a realism that reaches beyond construction toward a reality that exists whether or not we apprehend it.[3]

The challenge is to understand how such an ambiguity can be constructed and maintained in a work which exists as a verbal construction, acknowledges itself as such, and yet points beyond to something outside the realm of language. My approach will be through metaphor. To say that something is metaphoric is to imply that it is not literal but a similitude constructed through language. A strict constructivist position maintains that everything is metaphor, since in this view whatever we can speak or know is always already a representation, not reality as such. Yet to say that something is metaphoric is also to evoke the possibility of literal speech, since metaphor is a concept constructed through its difference from literal signification. Metaphor thus paradoxically provides a way to think about the literal and the metaphoric at the same time.

97

If one were to construct a metaphor that alluded to the literality hidden in the concept of metaphor, one would have a metaphor that was both self-reflexive (that is, referring to a class that includes itself as a member) and self-deconstructing (since by necessity it reveals its own hidden complement of literality). Metaphors that work on this double level I will call meta-metaphors.[4] The self-reflexive and self-deconstructive looping of meta-metaphors is essential to *The Crying of Lot 49*'s construction of its haunting ambiguities. Frank Palmeri made essentially the same point when he argued that *The Crying of Lot 49* can be understood as an attempt to construct a mode of representation that eludes the dichotomy between literal and metaphoric speech.[5] I believe that he is correct, although I want to take the argument in a different direction by referring to the important work on metaphor of Lakoff and Johnson in *Metaphors We Live By.*[6] Bear with me, then, as we take a detour through metaphor seen as the means by which we construct our world.

Lakoff and Johnson make a strong argument for a constructivist understanding of metaphor by demonstrating that so-called "dead" metaphors are very much alive, working to structure thought, direct action, and evoke emotion. As an example, they instance "argument is war."[7] The expression's martial thrust is reinscribed in the language we use to characterize arguments: strategies are planned, positions attacked or defended, claims demolished or established. Such language creates a conceptual framework that profoundly affects how we talk about argument, think about it, and how we actually argue. With war as the governing metaphor, argument is constructed as an activity that has winners and losers. Even relatively congenial arguments often become competitions governed by the desire to win. How different the situation would be, they suggest, if the governing metaphor were "argument is dance." Then the activity would be seen as a collaboration between partners rather than a competition, leading to very different behavior and emotions. The example illustrates that ordinary metaphors such as "argument is war" are not inevitable. They are cultural constructs, expressing the implicit values of the society that produces and is produced by them.

This approach to metaphor has more power than may at first

appear. It can be extended to explain why certain expressions and not others appear in a language. Consider the expression "I am up for the party." Lakoff and Johnson demonstrate that it is part of a cluster of phrases implying "up is good."[8] Another cluster of terms implies "front is good." An expression like "upfront" is possible because the values expressed by these two metaphoric clusters are coherent. "Downfront" or "upback" would not work in the same way because the values implicit in these expressions do not easily mesh. The joining of one cluster of values to another is an extension of how metaphors work in general. Metaphors map one set of experiences onto another, making it possible for us to understand each in terms of the other. Ordinary metaphors typically link a physically immediate action or sensation with a more abstract notion. If I say, "I am up for the party," I am comparing a complex emotional state with a spatial orientation grounded in everyday experience. If both parts of a metaphoric comparison were equally abstract, the metaphor would lose its anchor in immediate physical reality and thus much of its force. If both parts were equally immediate, the metaphor would be redundant.

Metaphoric coherence should not be confused with congruence. The joining of one cluster to another, like the mapping of a single concept onto another, is never an exact transposition. Some parts fit, others do not. Just as the "argument is war" metaphor hides the collaborative aspect of argument, so "upfront" hides the fact that holding back and lying low may be more appropriate strategies for some situations. Metaphors do not describe an objective reality, unmediated by a human perspective; rather, they help to construct the world in which we move. This does not mean that they should be avoided. Indeed it would be almost impossible to avoid them, for they are essential to human comprehension. How do we understand reality, except to compare one thing to another? Even seemingly objective measurements are comparisons that have metaphoric roots. If I say a room is five yards wide, for example, I am comparing it to a unit of measure representing the average length of an Anglo-Saxon girdle.[9] If I say the diameter of an atom is 8.34 angstroms, the basis for the comparison has changed, but there is still a comparison at the heart of the statement. Ordinary metaphors involve more elaborate structures than simple measurements, but they are like them in being comparisons. Any comparison, from a measurement of length to a highly wrought trope, suppresses some aspects of a phenomenon in order to bring others into view. Metaphors thus conceal as well as reveal, deconstructing some aspects of experience at the same time that they construct others.

The revolutionary thrust of Lakoff and Johnson's approach comes from their demonstration that expressions we have ceased to think of as metaphors nevertheless have the power to construct experience. The point about metaphoric coherence is important because it shows how metaphors connect with each other to form larger structures of thought; such a mechanism is necessary if metaphors are to have the constitutive force that Lakoff and Johnson claim for them. Although Lakoff and Johnson are primarily concerned with ordinary metaphors, their approach has significant implications for the artistic metaphors of *The Crying of Lot 49.* Especially illuminating is their emphasis on the conjunction of the concrete and the abstract in metaphors. Like less complex metaphoric structures, *The Crying of Lot 49* works by overlaying a physically immediate reality – Oedipa's quest through the parking lots, motels, bars, flophouses, and auction rooms of Southern California – onto another, more abstract series of junctions, crossings, and divergences grouped under the signifier "Tristero." The concreteness of the physical journey functions as an anchor for the metaphoric comparison, pointing toward the more abstract concept that is the object of Oedipa's quest. As things turn out, however, the object is not singular but multiple; the narrator calls the Tristero a "metaphor of God knew how many parts" (109). Moreover, in its broadest significance, the Tristero is not an object at all but a process. For as soon as it comes into view as a comprehensible object, it is converted into the concrete term of metaphoric joining that points to something more abstract. And when that more abstract concept comes into view, it in turn is converted into the concrete term of another metaphoric joining that points to something yet more abstract. This process constitutes the expansive aspect of Oedipa's quest, taking us to the verge of what cannot be spoken, but only gestured toward.

In ordinary metaphors, the arrow of meaning points mainly in one direction, from the concrete to the abstract. The concrete side of the comparison informs and shapes our conception of the abstract side. Artistic metaphors have greater license. They differ from ordinary metaphors chiefly in being less likely to follow in the grooves of customary usage. The difference is important, for it allows artistic metaphors to perform significantly different functions than do ordinary metaphors. In particular, artistic metaphors can, and often do, challenge and reorient customary perceptions rather than reinscribe them. In *The Crying of Lot 49,* this artistic license is exercised by having the metaphoric arrows point in both directions – sometimes from the concrete to the abstract, and sometimes from the abstract to the concrete. The expansive movement is thus paired with and balanced by a contracting movement, in which Oedipa slides from the abstract to the concrete side of metaphors. The process constitutes the reductive aspect of Oedipa's quest, pushing toward the literalization of language.

The force of metaphor in *The Crying of Lot 49* derives from a complex interplay between these expansive and reductive movements. By itself, the reductive movement would construct the Tristero as a historically specific entity with no significance beyond its existence as a conspiracy against Thurn and Taxis, turning *The Crying of Lot 49* into a mystery novel rather than a metaphysical inquiry.[10] Similarly, the expansive movement by itself would construct the Tristero as an increasingly remote abstraction with little or no efficacy in the world. Together, they create what might be called a two-cycle engine, whose motive power derives from the differential between the concrete and abstract polarities within metaphor. Pushed to the extreme, each movement of the cycle has the capacity to reverse itself and become the other, much like a piston that, having reached the maximum point of compression or expansion, begins to move in the opposite direction. But this is where the mechanical metaphor is transcended. An air of mystery surrounds the cusp points, which are often rendered as moments when the language becomes so compressed and dense, or so attenuated and rarefied, that it acquires the extraordinary power to reach beyond itself into its own ground of being. These transformative moments open a window on another order of reality and rescue the narrative from the tyranny of either/or. It is because of such moments that the Tristero, at once metaphoric and literal, can represent an exit from the "exitlessness" of contemporary America that Oedipa believes "harrows the head of every American you know," herself included (170).

Crossings between expansion and reduction happen throughout the text.[11] Yet there is also a narrative drift to the action of the novel. The first phase of Oedipa's quest is characterized by a general movement toward expansion; the second, toward contraction. At the cusp, when the outward expansion is halted and the inward contraction has not yet begun, there is an explosion of metaphor, as if all of the complicated crossings and junctions were for an instant overlaid upon one another. So dense is the language at this point, so rich in meditation about the nature of language and particularly metaphor, that it becomes a metaphor for metaphor itself. Then the meta-metaphoric nature of the text's tropes becomes explicit. This is the point toward which our inquiry will wend and where it will dwell the longest. Already, perhaps, I have said enough to demonstrate that metaphor is not merely ornamental to the language and structure of *The Crying of Lot 49*. Metaphor is at once the engine that drives the text, and the escape hatch out of the world constructed as a two-cycle engine. Constructing and deconstructing the world of *The Crying of Lot 49*, metaphor points to its own fundamentally ambiguous relation to the world we inhabit.

The starting point for our inquiry is the cluster of metaphors near the beginning of the novel that suggests Oedipa's comfortable suburban existence has wrapped her in a blanket of insulation. When Roseman attempts to play footsie with Oedipa under the lunch table, she finds that her boots prevent her from feeling much and so, "insulated, she decided not to make any fuss" (19). The incident serves as a trope for Oedipa's life before it is pierced by Inverarity's will. The Muzak in the supermarket surrounds Oedipa with musical ooze; the twilight cocktails she shares with Mucho and their well-intentioned failures to communicate suggest a marriage whose primary purpose is to insulate them from life and each other. The escapes offered Oedipa at this early point are worse than the vague sense of entrapment she feels: Mucho's agonized response to the used cars, Hilarius's LSD program, Roseman's proposal to go away to a destination he cannot even imagine.

Insulation is also a property of electrical and telephone wires, necessary to keep current and messages flowing. There are two telephone calls mentioned in this section, both occurring at the unearthly hour of 3:00 a.m. The first is Pierce's call, a potpourri of voices and coded messages ending in the promise of a visit from The Shadow, whose ghostly laughter was the hallmark of the radio program. The second is from Hilarius. At first these appear to be unrelated transmissions, insulated from one another. As Hilarius's name suggests, however, the two are connected through the complex interpretive possibilities offered by The Shadow. Either the Tristero is part of a plot concocted by Inverarity, meant to uncover its actual historical existence or simply to convince Oedipa it exists; or it is a Hilarius-like delusion, testifying to nothing save Oedipa's tendency toward paranoia and hallucinations. The twinning of the messages suggests that the insulation separating these possibilities will break down, allowing them to mix.

But first Oedipa must realize that she is insulated. This occurs in the well-known passage where she recalls the Remedios Varo painting of maidens imprisoned in a tower, spinning out into the void the tapestry that is the world (20–22).[12] The painting acts as a metaphor for more than Oedipa's life. The revelations she will have, the narrator asserts, are "[h]ardly about Pierce Inverarity, or herself; but about what remained yet had somehow, before this, stayed away. There had hung the sense of buffering, insulation, she had noticed the absence of an intensity, as if watching a movie, just perceptibly out of focus, that the projectionist refused to fix" (20). What happens when the insulation is stripped away, the picture brought into focus? On the one hand, it might lead to a more intimate contact with reality; on the other, that "reality" might itself be revealed as a construction, a tapestry spilling into the void. The difference is whether the insulation buffers Oedipa from reality as such, or from the knowledge that the only reality we ever know is that which we have constructed. In the first instance, there is a possibility that Oedipa can escape from the tower that insulates her from the world; in the second there is no such possibility, for there is nowhere to stand except on the ground of our own metaphoric fabrications. The ambiguity is crucial to the developing design of the text, haunting it until the final page.

In the next cluster of metaphors, the insulation begins to be stripped away. The ambiguity about whether this brings Oedipa closer to reality, or closer to realizing that we all play at constructing something we call reality, does not disappear, but intensifies. Oedipa, agreeing to play Strip Botticelli with Metzger, is surrounded by a sense that she is playing a role. She looks for stage lights when he appears at the door, thinking him so unnaturally handsome that he must be an actor. She soon finds out, as they watch *Cashiered* together, that he was in fact Baby Igor, a child actor. When she eventually acquiesces to having him undress her, "it took him 20 minutes, rolling, arranging her this way and that," as if "he were some scaled-up, short-haired, poker-faced little girl with a Barbie doll" (42). Stripped of her protective clothing, Oedipa still finds herself buffered from the reality of the encounter; she "may have fallen asleep once or twice" and "awoke at last to find herself getting laid" (42).

The ambiguity of the stripping process is amplified by the play on Narcissus and Echo that pervades this section.[13] Oedipa, like the nymph whose visage and name grace Echo Court, fears that she may be losing her corporeality when she looks in the bathroom mirror and sees nothing. In the heart-stopping moment it takes her to remember the mirror was broken by the hair spray can, she has time to wonder if Metzger will disappear when the sun comes up. Metzger, playing Narcissus to Oedipa's Echo, finds his reflection in the TV screen, but in a pinch the motel's reflecting pool and blank windows would also serve. Lest the reader skip over these clues, Pynchon reinforces them by setting the action in San Narciso and peppering the text with references to Saint Narcissus. Clearly Echo and Narcissus are in some way central to the design. As metaphors, they represent two opposed but related possibilities: on the one hand, being trapped like Narcissus in a solipsistic world that contains only the self and its reflections; on the other, dissipating outward like Echo until there is nothing left of the self. The pairing suggests that the alternative to entrapment is losing oneself altogether. One either stays on the tapestry one has woven or falls into the void.

There are similar pairings elsewhere. The next time Oedipa sees Hilarius, for example, he is in the grip of a paranoid delusion, caught in the prison of the self. The same evening she also sees Mucho and realizes that, high on LSD, he has dissipated into a "roomful of people." The two outcomes are linked not only on a literal level by the plot – it is Hilarius who gave Mucho the LSD – but thematically and metaphorically. Hilarius cannot escape from the past, as if time never moved; Mucho is convinced that "time is arbitrary," and you can "pick your zero point anywhere you want, that way you can shuffle each person's time line sideways till they all coincide" (142). Although representing opposite choices, the fates of Hilarius and Mucho are metaphorically coherent in Lakoff and Johnson's sense; they share the basic premise that there is only the tower and the void. This coherence explains why the two seemingly antithetical possibilities are sometimes combined into a single trope. Oedipa suspects, for example, that the Paranoids and their girlfriends are somehow "plugging in" to her and Metzger's orgasms, in an odd combination of paranoid intensity and Mucho-like dissipation.

The stripping metaphor connects this early phase of Oedipa's quest with her introduction to the Tristero. After meeting Mike Fallopian at the Scope (whose name links him to Oedipa's later intuition that she is pregnant with something the gynecologist has no test for), Oedipa witnesses an underground mail system at work and sees the muted post horn emblem on the bathroom wall. The narrator uses the extended metaphor of the Tristero as a burlesque stripper to characterize Oedipa's initiation into the conspiracy. Like Oedipa's Strip Botticelli, the Tristero's striptease is sexually suggestive, but the stakes in this game are something other than pleasure:

> As if the breakaway gowns, net bras, jeweled garters and G-strings of historical figuration that would fall away were layered dense as Oedipa's own streetclothes in that game with Metzger in front of the Baby Igor movie; as if a plunge toward dawn indefinite black hours long would indeed be necessary before The Tristero could be revealed in its terrible nakedness. Would its smile, then, be coy, and would it flirt away harmlessly backstage, say good night with a Bourbon Street bow and leave her in peace? Or would it instead,

the dance ended, come back down the runway, its luminous stare locked to Oedipa's, smile gone malign and pitiless; bend to her alone among the desolate row of seats and begin to speak words she never wanted to hear? (54)

"Historical figuration" is here only a covering, to be stripped away in a performance that will reveal the Tristero's "terrible naked-ness."[14] Bound up with the suggestion that reality lies behind or apart from history is the hint that the performance will be more than just a show. Crossing the boundary between art and life, the Tristero touches Oedipa through the message it will deliver, the words it will speak that "she never wanted to hear." Not historical fact, then, but language so potent it must be gestured toward rather than rendered in the reality that underlies the expansive aspect of Oedipa's quest. This is one of the places where the Tristero, at first the more abstract term in a metaphoric comparison, slides into the position of the concrete term so that it can point to something even more abstract – something that can be indicated but not articulated.

Yet there are also places when the reductive movement is apparent. The twinning of the two movements parallels the interconversion of life and art. Life becoming art moves toward abstraction, art becoming life toward literalization. Oedipa feels that her encounter with Metzger is like playing a role in a movie, but the movie that they watch together is eerily real. During a battle scene, Metzger recalls that for "fifty yards out the sea was red with blood. They don't show that" (36). An actor-turned-lawyer, Metzger claims to have had a TV pilot based on his career, with the lead played by Manny Di Presso, a lawyer-turned-actor. No doubt it is significant that the trope of art becoming life, already conventional by the time of the Renaissance, is constructed in *The Crying of Lot 49* by emphasizing the performative aspects of the legal profession. The construction hints that the legal world Oedipa entered when she was named executrix of Pierce's will is not a clear-cut world of fact. Rather it is a twilight zone populated by people like Metzger, Di Presso, and Roseman, the lawyer who spends his time writing *The Profession v. Perry Mason, A Not-so-hypothetical Indictment* (19). If we readers are the jury that is to decide Oedipa's case – as the suspended judgment of the ending suggests – the trope makes clear that the decision can be based on no simple black-and-white distinctions between the metaphoric and the literal, art and life.

By the time Oedipa gets around to attending a performance of *The Courier's Tragedy,* these tropes have prepared us to see the play as more than casually related to the "real" events of the plot. In a reality built of language, words have a power of action and transformation not easily imagined in less verbally constructed realms. The play continues to inscribe ambiguous pairs of possibilities. The movement toward reduction is signified by the stripping away of hope from life, life from bodies, bodies from bones that in turn are ground to make ink. But here the movement toward reduction is turned inside out, for the ink is fluid, subject to dispersal into messages that can be transformed and reinterpreted. So when the evil Pasquale has the bones of murdered men ground into ink that he then uses to write a lying message meant to save his life, the message is transformed into a revelation of his crimes and an exoneration of his victim. The cusp, the point of maximum compression where reduction paradoxically turns into dispersal, is marked by the Word.

These patterns reappear in various forms throughout the text. For example, the bones of the murdered GIs that lie at the bottom of Lago di Pieta represent a cusp point of reduction. The bones are "harvested" by Tony Jaguar, a metaphor that likens them to the dandelions that grow on the graves plowed up for the San Narciso Freeway and harvested to make the wine that Genghis Cohen offers Oedipa. The wine grows cloudy in spring, as "if the dead really do persist, even in a bottle of wine" (99). Once harvested, the bones are transported to the United States and joined with bones from the very same San Narciso cemetery, which are then put to a variety of uses, including serving as decorative objects at the bottom of Fangoso Lagoons. There they are ready to become part of the message Inverarity sends Oedipa from beyond the grave, "as if the dead really do persist." As in *The Courier's Tragedy,* reduction and dispersal are signified through bones and fluids, with the point of reversal marked by a message of transformative power.

When Oedipa tries to pin things down and locate a source for the emerging patterns she senses, she finds that her attempts to reduce complexity only result in more dispersion. Visiting the director-actor Randolph Driblette after the performance, she is greeted by eyes "surrounded by an incredible network of lines, like a laboratory maze for studying intelligence in tears" (77). The trope recalls Oedipa weeping before the Varo painting of the tapestry spilling from the tower. Then, she wondered if her bubble shades would fill up and she would continue to "see the world refracted through those tears, those specific tears, as if indices as yet unfound varied in important ways from cry to cry" (21). If there is intelligence in those tears, Driblette would be an appropriate person to study them. Reiterating the theme of the Varo painting, he insists that the life he gave the play came from his own mind, not from any text that can be reproduced and transmitted. Moreover, he asserts that his motive for interpreting Wharfinger's words as he did is ultimately unknowable. The "reality," he claims, "is in *this* head. Mine. I'm the projector at the planetarium, all the closed little universe visible in the circle of that stage is coming out of my mouth, eyes, sometimes other orifices also" (79). Like the tapestry the imprisoned maidens weave, the world he projects has no external referent other than the inexplicable workings of his mind. The connection proves to be as fragile as it is mysterious, for Driblette later disappears into the Pacific Ocean, a fate foreshadowed by his shower water dribbling down the drain.

If the ocean disperses, it also cleanses. Oedipa is drawn to the ocean partly because she imagines it is so vast that it can retain its purity despite all of the contaminants humans dump into it. She even imagines that the ocean may, in some mysterious way, be the salvation of southern California. Unlike the land, it remains unmarked and unfurrowed. In this respect it contrasts with the California landscapes where Oedipa, looking down on suburban tracts and freeway mazes, thinks she detects "a hieroglyphic sense of concealed meaning, of an intent to communicate" (24). The feeling is associated especially with San Narciso, where Oedipa senses "a revelation" that "trembled just past the threshold of her understanding," as if "at the centre of an odd, religious instant. As if, on some other frequency, or out of the eye of some whirlwind rotating too slow for her heated skin even to feel the centrifugal coolness of, words were being spoken" (24–5).[15]

This hieroglyphic landscape, redolent with the Word, is repeatedly associated with electronic circuits, as if the marks on the land turned it into a giant computer. The metaphoric conjunction of a computer with an ineffable religious experience may seem strange; but it is consistent with the tendency of reduction and dissipation to turn themselves inside out at moments of greatest intensity. The dynamic is characteristic of Oedipa's quest. Indeed, it provides the quest's emotional tension as well as its underlying structure. When it seems that the clues are about to dissipate into thin air, a reversal takes place and more concrete leads appear. When matters threaten to become too concrete and clear-cut, they undergo a reversal and begin to dissipate. The dynamic is more than a way to keep the narrative going and the suspense tight, although that is one of its functions. The deeper purpose is to constitute and sustain a question that emerges with increasing clarity as Oedipa approaches the bifurcation point where her quest will undergo a phase change.

One way this question is posed is through WASTE. Is it a word, as Oedipa first pronounces it to Stanley Koteks, or an acronym? If it is a word, then the assorted weirdos that Oedipa meets are only waste, the detritus of a society that will discard them like so many used sanitary napkins. If it is an acronym, a signifier underwritten by other signifiers, then the pieces add up to something more than a jumble of misfits. The reductive process points toward the word, the dissipative toward the diffusion into other signifiers. But since each can turn into the other and carries some of the other's values with it, the question cycles around, growing more complex and encompassing more tropes, without ever being definitively answered. The question is crucial because it is not merely the status of the misfits that is at issue. The state of America is, too, for if there is no meaning to those who do not fit into the accepted grooves, no hope that they offer alternatives, then the narrative can run only in the furrows that already mark the land and the language. In a profound sense, this outcome would mean that the metaphors of the text had failed.

How is the question to be decided? The text offers various approaches; one is through the Nefastis Machine. On a literal level, if Oedipa can succeed in getting the piston to move, it may indicate that John Nefastis is something more than a cracked inventor. Evidently the experiment's significance goes beyond this, however, for Oedipa is close to tears when it fails. On a metaphoric level, the Nefastis Machine functions as a trope for the connection between dissipation and reduction, the basis for which lies in the history of thermodynamics and information theory. Its gist is presented by Nefastis when he explains to Oedipa that there are two kinds of entropy – one from thermodynamics, another from information theory (104–8).[16]

The Nefastis Machine illustrates how Pynchon creates tropes out of diverse materials and uses them to constitute the larger design of the text. Thermodynamic entropy is a measure of the amount of heat lost for useful purposes in a heat exchange. The second law of thermodynamics states that in a closed system, entropy always tends to increase. This means, in effect, that the universe is constantly running down (assuming it is a closed system). According to scenarios constructed by nineteenth-century thermodynamicists, the process will stop only when there are no heat reservoirs left anywhere, at which point the temperature will stabilize close to absolute zero (minus 273 degrees centigrade) and life of any kind will be impossible. Lord Kelvin, the distinguished British thermodynamicist, was among the first to articulate this scenario when in 1852 he characterized the second law as a "universal tendency to the dissipation of mechanical energy."[17] Thermodynamic entropy, then, is akin to the dissipating processes in *The Crying of Lot 49*, pointing toward an attenuation whose end point is the cessation of life.

As Nefastis explains, thermodynamic entropy is connected to information through Maxwell's Demon. Maxwell's Demon was part of a thought experiment devised by James Clerk Maxwell to test the second law of thermodynamics.[18] Maxwell imagined a box full of gas, divided in half by a partition in which there was a hole with a shutter. Suppose, Maxwell said, that a small being (later called a demon) sits atop this frictionless shutter and uses it to open or close the hole. When a fast molecule approaches the hole, the demon allows it to pass through. When a slow one comes, he closes the shutter. Through this mechanism, there will soon be more fast molecules on one side than the other. Since molecular speed correlates with temperature, there will also be a temperature differential between the sides, which can be used to do work without having had to put any work into the system. Earlier, when Stanley Koteks was explaining Nefastis's invention, Oedipa had objected that the demon's sorting is work, using the post office as an example (86). Koteks is correct in saying that the demon's sorting is not considered work in the thermodynamic sense; because the shutter is frictionless, it can be moved without the expenditure of work. Oedipa's objection, however, hints at the solution to the conundrum that evolved through nearly a century of commentary. The crucial point was not the work performed in moving the shutter, but the information needed to carry out the sorting operation.

In 1951, Leon Brillouin argued that the flaw in the experiment lay in the assumption that the demon knew which were the slow and fast molecules.[19] Brillouin showed that to complete his sorting, the demon would have to have some way to "see" the molecules, and that the energy he expended to do so would be more than the energy created by the sorting process. The immediate result of Brillouin's argument was to vindicate the second law. A more important implication (since the second law was never really in doubt) was that there was a connection between information and entropy. Because he constituted the connection through Maxwell's Demon, Brillouin naturally thought that information and entropy should be opposites. The more information the demon gained, the less entropy there was in the box; the less information, the more entropy. Claude Shannon disagreed. Often called the father of modern information theory, Shannon used entropy and information as interchangeable terms, as if they were the same thing. Thus Nefastis tells Oedipa that no one is sure how thermodynamic and informational entropy are related.

The debate between Brillouin and Shannon marked a turning point in how entropy was conceptualized.[20] In Shannon's view, systems rich in entropy are not simply poor in order; rather, they are rich in information. The key is to think of disorder as maximum information. So influential has this view become that in contemporary irreversible thermodynamics, entropy is seen as an engine driving systems toward increasing complexity rather than dissolution.[21] In cosmology, it has recently been used to construct a model of the universe that does not end in heat death, because entropy bestows upon it the capacity to renew itself.[22] How much of this material Pynchon knew when he wrote *The Crying of Lot 49* is unclear; some of it has appeared since then. Nevertheless, his first important published work was "Entropy," a short story that juxtaposed the sterility of an ordered closed system with the chaotic vitality of an open system.[23] The existence of this story suggests that several years before he wrote *The Crying of Lot 49*, Pynchon had already sensed that disorder, conceived as maximum information rather than dissipation, could offer an exit from the traditional "exitlessness" of heat death scenarios.

This is the background of the Nefastis Machine. Apparently the purpose of the machine is to literalize the connection between information and entropy by converting information directly into mechanical energy. "Communication is the key," Nefastis cries (105). Significantly, there is a disproportionate relation between energy and information in Nefastis's scheme. Just as a very small amount of mass is converted to an enormous amount of energy in Einstein's famous equation $E = mc^2$, so in the Nefastis Machine a huge amount of information is necessary to create a tiny amount of energy. "One little movement," Nefastis signs, "against all that massive complex of information, destroyed over and over with each power stroke" (106). Whereas *The Crying of Lot 49* uses information to create a verbal engine that can drive toward transformation, Nefastis's machine destroys information to create a trivial mechanical movement. The Nefastis Machine is thus a demonic version of the two-cycle engine that drives the novel. Moreover, if the Nefastis Machine could work, its success would imply that the differential between the metaphoric and literal that Pynchon uses to fuel his machine does not in fact exist. Nefastis calls entropy a "figure of speech . . . a metaphor. It connects the world of thermodynamics to the world of information flow. The Machine uses both. The Demon makes the metaphor not only verbally graceful, but also objectively true" (106). With the collapse of the metaphoric into the literal, the cycling between dissipation and reduction that constitutes the metaphoric structure of *The Crying of Lot 49* would be reduced to a merely mechanical process – and a trivial one at that.

But of course the machine doesn't work. When Oedipa runs screaming from the "hippy-dippy" Nefastis after he proposes that they "do it" on the couch while watching the evening news (107–8), the potential for transformation is left intact. Nevertheless, the encounter with the Nefastis Machine leaves its mark upon the subsequent narration. It makes explicit the connection between thermodynamics and information theory, thus laying the groundwork for a corresponding connection between heat machines and computers. Heat engines operate on cycles of expansion and compression, computers on binary circuitry; in this sense both are double-valued deterministic systems. The Nefastis Machine, understood as a demented attempt to escape universal heat death, also acts as a subtle reminder that whatever transformations language can effect, human beings remain bound to a world of irreversible processes in which death is inevitable. Both binary determinism and irreversibility loom large in the reductive phase of Oedipa's quest. At the cusp, they intermingle with metaphor to create a passage of extraordinary complexity and intensity.

The cusp arrives after Oedipa's night of drifting through the streets of San Francisco. Willing to go where chance takes her, she has found signs of the Tristero everywhere. As dawn breaks she feels beat-up, saturated with information, confronted with evidence she cannot dismiss. If the Tristero is her fantasy, it has grown to such gargantuan proportions that she must seriously entertain the prospect that she is crazy. If it really exists, it implies that an alternative world lies side-by-side with conventional reality, touching, interpenetrating, yet still maintaining its separate identity. Whatever she chooses to believe, she can no longer dismiss the Tristero as irrelevant or trivial. With this realization she encounters the old sailor, and the text's language grows as densely saturated as her experiences the night before.

Separated from his wife, the sailor is "shaking with grief" (125). Oedipa imagines his trembling as a shaking loose from ordinary society, supposing him "[c]ammed each night out of that safe furrow the bulk of this city's waking each sunrise again set virtuously to plowing" (125–6). Presumably the sailor has spent his working life on the unmarked ocean that the narrator earlier contrasted with the furrowed land. Now the sailor is released from the city's "safe furrow" not by his vocation, but by a metaphor drawn from mechanics. A cam is an off-center rod driven by a flywheel. It is eccentric in the literal sense of being away from the center; the metaphor ties its eccentricity to the sailor's marginal position in society. Oddly, this cam works not in a machine but in a "furrow." The conjunction of the mechanical and the agricultural, like the imprinting of a computer circuitboard on the landscape, implicitly juxtaposes an idyllic American past with a troubled present and problematic future.[24] In its earlier manifestations, this metaphoric conjunction signified concern about what America means and where it is going. The sailor is an object of Oedipa's and the narrator's attention because, "unfurrowed" by trade and loss, he might possess a privileged viewpoint that can answer these questions. The problem is how to get in touch with his knowledge. The medium of communication is significantly not speech, which seems always to fall short of ultimate revelation in this text, but, grotesquely, the soiled rented mattress on which he sleeps.[25] Oedipa thinks of the desperate old men who have slept upon the mattress and the bodily fluids sweated into it, "like the memory bank to a computer of the lost" (126). Crossing the threshold between observation and participation, she comes up the last three steps and holds the sailor, not only to comfort but also to come into deeper communication with him.

Her sympathy draws her into the flophouse to the sailor's cubicle, where she sees the stained mattress she had envisioned. She imagines it going up in flames in a "Viking's funeral," set on fire by a cigarette the sailor let drop (128). Then the "set of all men who had slept on it, whatever their lives had been, would truly cease to be, forever, when the mattress burned" (128). So it is not lost knowledge that finally comes to Oedipa, but the realization of loss itself. "She stared at it in wonder. It was if she had just discovered the irreversible process" (128). Irreversibility, a concept from thermodynamics, denotes a process in which entropy is produced. The allusion implicitly connects the human world of death and loss with the thermodynamic scenario of universal heat death.

Oedipa's realization that the sailor will die is the logical sequel to her earlier failure to communicate with Maxwell's Demon and "keep it all cycling." Like Pierce's injunction to "keep it bouncing" (178), Nefastis's dream had a nefarious untruth at its center – the maniacal belief that enough motion, enough information fed into the system, can somehow allow one to escape death. The destruction of information in the sailor's mattress signifies what is lost when the human spirit is extinguished. The total of mass and energy may remain constant, but the delicate webs that connect neurons to thoughts, electrons to memory and feeling, are gone forever. The moment signals a profound turning point in the text. After this encounter, Oedipa will seem less interested in seeking an elusive and possibly illusory Tristero than in wearily recognizing its inevitability. The expansive phase of her quest is almost at an end. In the reductive phase, the issue is not so much the possibilities that the Tristero opens up as the choices it demands.

In a final explosion of metaphor, the narrator turns his attention to the delirium tremens from which the sailor suffers (was the earlier trembling really from grief?). He interprets the DTs as "a metaphor, a trembling unfurrowing of the mind's plowshare" (128). As always with metaphors of furrows and plows, the subterranean current of thought leads into America's past, this time to the Puritan fascination with the Word.[26] The clairvoyant, the paranoid, and the dreamer "all act in the same special relevance to the word, or whatever it is the word is there, buffering, to protect us from" (129). The language recalls the sense of insulation that surrounded Oedipa at the beginning of her quest, but now the text cannot strip the buffer away, for it is language itself. The textual signifiers have taken us as far as they can; what lies beyond can be pointed toward, but not articulated.

What then are metaphors? "A thrust at truth and a lie," the narrator says in one of the text's most enigmatic passages, "depending on where you were: inside, safe, or outside, lost" (129). One way to interpret the comment is to think of "inside" as inside the furrow, surrounded by Muzak and supermarkets with beaded curtains. "Outside" would then be among the detritus, kin to the sailor and all the other outcasts and misfits Oedipa has encountered on her quest. The syntax links "inside" with metaphors as a "thrust at truth," "outside" with them as "a lie." If it were the other way around, the passage would be easier to understand. To think of metaphors as a lie is to dismiss them, and therefore to decline the quest constituted through them. To accept that they can be a "thrust at truth" is to accept the quest and to encounter the Tristero, the text's central metaphor. But this is not what the syntax implies. What are we to make of the other, syntactically stronger reading?

For those inside, metaphors may be a thrust at truth because they hint at the constructed nature of reality; for those outside, they are a lie because like any other language, they cannot penetrate the construction to touch reality as such. The double readings, one suggesting that language can point toward ultimate reality and the other insisting that it must always fall short, point to a fundamental ambiguity. Although the text's language acknowledges that its constructions do not constitute reality as such, there is an intense desire at critical points to drive beyond language, to rip through it to what lies behind. Hence the stripping metaphors and the evocation of a space that lies beyond the tapestry. In the expansive phase, the Tristero is a signifier for this desire. It stands for taking the risk of jumping off the world as it is consensually constituted. But as Tristero emerges from the shadows into actuality, it necessarily enters into the theater of representation and thus loses its power to signify beyond. Precisely because it can be talked about, it is not that which lies beyond language. As soon as the taboo of silence that Driblette imposed on the word in *The Courier's Tragedy* is broken, the Tristero as metaphor begins to dribble away, replaced by the Tristero as historical reality.

The passage about the mattress shows the same ambiguity at work. The text constructs the mattress as a material object, saturated with bodily fluids whose chemistry is encoded with the history of the sailor as a physical being who sweats, urinates, ejaculates. At the same time, of course, the mattress is a verbal structure, as the text acknowledges when it is used metaphorically to anticipate the sailor's death. Likening the burning mattress to a "Viking's funeral," this metaphoric construction evokes the loss of the mattress as object, and with it the loss of the information that defined the sailor as a living being. The metaphoric reading points toward dispersal, the literal toward contraction and recuperation. At this moment of turning, both senses are strongly present. Intermingling and interpenetrating, they signify loss as well as retrieval, connection as well as alienation.

It is no wonder that Oedipa, "trembling, unfurrowed" on the cusp between expansion and reduction, "did not know where she was" (129). As she "sipped sidewise, screeching back across grooves of years" (129), the metaphoric crossings from plow to groove to phonograph record (another passage from agriculture to technology) take her to the differential calculus which the narrator interprets as an attempt to transform time into timelessness and, hence, implicitly to deny the human reality of death. The "high magic of low puns" links the sailor's DTs with dt understood as a time differential, a "vanishing small instant in which change had to be confronted at last for what it was, where it could no longer disguise itself as something innocuous like an average rate" (129).

The conjunction hints that the text's desire to go beyond language, to reach a realm beyond time and space, may, like calculus, have deep connections with the desire to deny death. It thus points to an affinity between the text in its expansive phase and the Nefastis Machine. If conjuring up the Nefastis Machine was meant as an exorcism, a casting out of a demon that also had power over the text itself, this passage reveals why the exorcism was necessary. Significantly, the connection is made through a pun rather than a metaphor. Puns have traditionally been considered "low" because they play on trivial or accidental correspondences. But what if the belief that these correspondences are trivial stems from an ideology that wishes to deny the correspondences that puns reveal? In that case puns, far from being exercises in bad taste, become instruments of revelation, exposing what "they" want to keep hidden. Moreover, this particular pun hints that "they" are in fact "we." This is the deeper purpose to the punning language of *The Crying of Lot 49* — to excavate connections that we would deny but that form the substrata of our beliefs and desires. Because a pun does not require the abstract/concrete differential that drives the metaphors of *The Crying of Lot 49,* it can work at moments when that dynamics has most called itself into question. When the self-reflexivity of meta-metaphors threatens to plunge us into a laby-

117

rinth of infinite recursion, puns come to the rescue to carry the language to further revelations.

In Oedipa's encounter with the sailor, a window opens onto an order of being beyond language, accessible only in vision. "She knew that the sailor had seen worlds no other man had seen . . . because DT's must give access to dt's of spectra beyond the known sun, music made purely of Antarctic loneliness and fright" (129). Through holding him, physically participating in his unfurrowed trembling, she has some intimation of what these other worlds might be. At the same time, the mortality of his visions is stressed; "nothing she knew of would preserve them, or him" (129). The double message is clear: vision is possible, death is inevitable. It illuminates why both expansion and reduction are necessary. Without reduction, expansion could continue into a megalomania that thinks it can deny death; without expansion, reduction leads to despair and a perverse drive toward inevitable death. Both expansion and reduction are required to keep W.A.S.T.E. from turning into trash.[27]

Before the reductive phase takes hold in earnest, Oedipa is granted a vision of what Jesus Arrabal might call "an anarchist miracle" (132). Joining a convention of deaf-mutes by chance and then whisked onto the dance floor, she sees each couple dancing to "whatever was in each fellow's head" (131). Yet there are no collisions; each couple's movements fits gracefully into the whole. The sign makes Oedipa think that there could be "some unthinkable order of music, many rhythms, all keys at once, a choreography in which each couple meshed easy, predestined. Something they all heard with an extra sense atrophied in herself" (131). The harmonious yet diverse dance can be seen as a trope for what America could have been, "with the chance once so good for diversity" (181). Significantly happening beyond language, in a silent semiotics of unheard music akin to the sailor's vision but without the loneliness, it trills a grace note of freedom before the major chord of reduction is struck.

Now begins the process of stripping down. In contrast to stripping away, stripping down reduces rather than expands Oedipa's options. Hilarius goes crazy, Mucho flips out, Metzger runs off with a teenager, Zapf's bookstore burns, the previously shy Genghis

Cohen floods Oedipa with information, even Mike Fallopian changes. As disturbing as any of these changes is the reification of the Tristero into a historical phenomenon, with its own leaders, internal dissensions, and accommodations.[28] In the conjectural history that Emory Bortz constructs, the Tristero at one point even considers *subsidizing* a weakened Thurn and Taxis. Some in the Tristero are afraid that if their traditional enemy collapses, their own opposition will cease to have purpose or meaning. The incident is a parable of co-optation. In this collapse of opposites into each other, the danger is that there may finally be no difference between conventional reality and the Tristero.

Another parable of co-optation is presented through the Scurvhamites, the Puritan sect thought to have published the obscene illustrated edition of *The Courier's Tragedy.* Believing that Creation was a "vast, intricate machine," part of which was run by God and part by a figure called the Antagonist, the "few saved Scurvhamites found themselves looking out into the gaudy clockwork of the doomed with a certain sick and fascinated horror, and this was to prove fatal" (155). One by one, the "glamorous prospect of annihilation coaxed them over" (155). These parables illustrate that, if we think of the text only as a two-cycle engine, reduction and expansion may be subsumed into a "gaudy clockwork" mechanism that is entirely deterministic. Then, like the Scurvhamites, we may become so fascinated with its mechanics that the cusp points can no longer function as a paradoxical release. What is needed is a delicate balance that allows one to recognize the inevitability of death without falling victim to despair.

As if to accentuate the danger, the imagery shows a decreasing range of options in a computerized landscape. "For it was now like walking among matrices of a great digital computer, the zeroes and ones twinned above, hanging like balanced mobiles right and left, ahead, thick, maybe endless" (181). The reductive process gradually excludes the middle range until there are four, then only two choices left, "one and zero," meaning or non-meaning:

> Ones and zeroes. So did the couples arrange themselves. At Vesperhaven House either an accommodation reached, in some kind of dignity, with the Angel of Death, or only death and the daily, tedious

preparations for it. Another mode of meaning behind the obvious, or none. Either Oedipa in the orbiting ecstasy of a true paranoia, or a real Tristero. For there either was some Tristero beyond the appearance of the legacy of America, or there was just America and if there was just America then it seemed the only way she could continue, and manage to be at all relevant to it, was as an alien, unfurrowed, assumed full circle into some paranoia. (182)

Oedipa, originally frightened of the Tristero, now realizes that it has become so essential to her that if it does not exist, she will be forced to invent it. She cannot simply fall back into the groove where she began. "Unfurrowed," she will remain so, even if it means retreating into an invented world of her own.

As the choices narrow, perhaps to the vanishing point, the text withdraws from the metaphysical thrust toward the absolute and turns toward a humane and compassionate interpretation of the Tristero. With its "constant theme" of disinheritance (160), it seems to signify the dispossessed everywhere – children in freight trains, homeless people sleeping in junked cars. Then, as the list continues, the narrator's examples turn increasingly toward language that does not communicate, messages that miss the human reality struggling to survive amid technical apparatus: people sleeping among telephone and telegraph wires, "living in the very copper rigging and secular miracle of communication, untroubled by the dumb voltages flickering their miles, the night long, in the thousands of unheard messages," drifters who speak their native tongue "as if they were in exile from somewhere else invisible yet congruent with the cheered land she lived in," callers who dial telephone numbers at random hoping for the "magical Other who would reveal herself out of the roar of relays, monotone litanies of insult, filth, fantasy" (180). The unvoiced but implicit concern is that *The Crying of Lot 49* itself, in its reach toward what lies beyond language, may miss the human reality that lies within its expressive power.[29]

As the text draws to a close, signs that the reductive phase is about to turn expansive increase. Now, however, the barest hint of a cusp point emerges. The strenuous task of construction and deconstruction, interpretation and constraint, falls to the reader rather than to the narrator. Edward Mendelson has pointed out that the auction resembles a sacred ritual.[30] He connects it to a famous hierophany in the Christian tradition, the Pentecost, when the Holy Ghost manifested itself as tongues of fire and caused the assembled faithful to speak in unknown languages. This final evocation of a transcendent meaning suggests that the reductive movement, pushed to the extreme, has swung back toward hierophany. The allusion to speaking in unknown tongues hints at the danger in this turn, as do the "pale cruel faces"of men in the room (183). What human price will the thrust toward the absolute extract? On the other hand, not to hazard it, to be content with staying in the groove, has become for Oedipa unthinkable. The Pentecost occurred fifty days after Christ died; that numerology offers the most plausible explanation for the "49" of the title. That the text stops just short of fifty clearly implies that it *cannot* answer its own central question – whether there is a hidden reality behind the surface of our lives, or just the surface. The truce the text finally has to offer is not unequivocal revelation, but necessary equivocation.

The argument I have pursued here, that the ambiguities preventing any clear-cut resolution of *The Crying of Lot 49* have a coherent structure of expansion and reduction, should not be confused with the claim that the text is logically consistent throughout. I use coherence in Lakoff and Johnson's sense – a structure that allows for slippages as well as for connection, for mappings that never exactly coincide, for comparisons that partially fit and partially do not. In my view, there really is a mystery to *The Crying of Lot 49*. The text cannot quite make up its mind whether its "verbally graceful" metaphors can reach a reality beyond language, and more fundamentally, cannot resolve whether the endeavor to do so is insane or inspired, divine or demonic. Thus the values assigned to the Tristero keep changing – sometimes menacing, sometimes comforting; sometimes metaphysical abstraction, sometimes historical conspiracy; sometimes illusory, sometimes real. Underlying these uncertainties is the profoundly ambiguous relationship of the text to its own language. Interrogating the conditions of possibility for its utterances, it is never able to resolve whether its language play is a postmodern excursion into consensual constructions or a thrust through the theater curtain to a higher order of reality, in which we may, after all, be mere playthings. Either possibility has its chances for joy and despair, grief and liberation. The only unthinkable option is not to question, to remain insulated within placid acceptances.

NOTES

1. For a reading of the ambiguous ending that connects it to the new physics, see Lance Olsen, "Pynchon's New Nature: The Uncertainty Principle in *The Crying of Lot 49*," *Canadian Review of American Studies* 14 (1983): 153–63. John P. Leland in "Pynchon's Linguistic Demon: *The Crying of Lot 49*," *Critique* 16 (1974): 45–53, exemplifies a postmodern reading of the novel. A more moderate position is taken by Robert Merrill in "The Form and Meaning of Pynchon's *The Crying of Lot 49*," *Ariel* 8 (1977): 53–71; Merrill argues for strong structural elements along with a postrealistic form.

2. This aspect of the novel has been noticed by many, including Robert Murray Davis in "Parody, Paranoia, and the Dead End of Language in *The Crying of Lot 49*," *Genre* 5 (1972): 367–77.

3. Frank Palmeri makes a similar point in "Neither Literally Nor as Metaphor: Pynchon's *The Crying of Lot 49* and the Structure of Scientific Revolutions," *ELH* 54 (1987): 979–99.

4. I am indebted to conversations with Nancy Barta Smith for these ideas about the literal and the metaphoric, and especially for the term "meta-metaphor."

5. Palmeri, "Neither Literally Nor as Metaphor." Palmeri sees *The Crying of Lot 49* as a paradigm-breaking text, working through a series of models that it deconstructs by proving their constitutive terms inadequate. Among the frames Palmeri considers are information theory and thermodynamics, narcissism, and genre.

6. George Lakoff and Mark Johnson, *Metaphors We Live By* (Chicago: University of Chicago Press, 1980).

7. Ibid., pp. 3–6.

8. Ibid., pp. 14–21.

9. I am indebted for this example, and for the point about the metaphoric basis of measurement, to F. C. McGrath's unpublished manuscript, "How Metaphor Works: What Boyle's Law and Shakespeare's 73rd Sonnet Have in Common."

10. Stefano Tani has written about *The Crying of Lot 49* as an anti-detective

novel in "The Dismemberment of the Detective," *Diogenes* 120 (1981): 22–41.

11. Robert Murray Davis uses a similar set of terms in "Parody, Paranoia, and the Dead End of Language," namely, "expansion" and "enclosure." He does not, however, use them as constitutive of Oedipa's quest in the same way I do.

12. David Cowart has an informative discussion of the centrality of Varo's work to *The Crying of Lot 49* in "Pynchon's *The Crying of Lot 49* and the Paintings of Remedios Varo," *Critique* 14 (1972): 19–26.

13. Many readers have noticed these usages. See Palmeri, "Neither Literally Nor As Metaphor" for a recounting of three different treatments of narcissism – Ovidean, Christian, and Freudian.

14. C. E. Nicholson and R. W. Stevenson discuss Pynchon's simultaneous reliance on and undercutting of history in "'Words You Never Wanted to Hear': History and Narratology in *The Crying of Lot 49*," in *Tropic Crucible: Self and Theory in Language and Literature*, ed. Ranjit Chatterjee and Colin Nicholson (Singapore: Singapore University Press, 1984), pp. 297–316. Tony Tanner also comments on the sense of history as theater in his contribution to *Thomas Pynchon: Modern Critical Views*, ed. Harold Bloom (New York: Chelsea House, 1986), pp. 175–89.

15. Edward Mendelson in "The Sacred, the Profane, and *The Crying of Lot 49*," *Thomas Pynchon: A Collection of Critical Essays*, ed. Edward Mendelson (Englewood Cliffs, N.J.: Prentice-Hall, 1978), pp. 112–46, has written on the "hierophanies" of the novel, connecting them to the work of Mircea Eliade and to the Pentecost.

16. Several readers have written on entropy in *The Crying of Lot 49*, including Leland, "Pynchon's Linguistic Demon"; Anne Mangel, "Maxwell's Demon, Entropy, Information: *The Crying of Lot 49*," in *Mindful Pleasures: Essays on Thomas Pynchon*, ed. George Levine and David Leverenz (Boston: Little, Brown, 1976), pp. 87–100; Peter L. Abernathy, "Entropy in Pynchon's *The Crying of Lot 49*," *Critique* 14 (1972): 18–33; William M. Plater, *The Grim Phoenix: Reconstructing Thomas Pynchon* (Bloomington: Indiana University Press, 1978), pp. 1–63, 220–4; and David Simberloff, "Entropy, Information and Life: Biophysics in the Novels of Thomas Pynchon," *Perspectives in Biology and Medicine* 21 (1978): 617–25.

17. William Thompson (Lord Kelvin), *Mathematical and Physical Papers*, vol. 1 (Cambridge: Cambridge University Press, 1981), p. 514.

18. A history of Maxwell's Demon can be found in W. Ehrenberg, "Maxwell's Demon," *Scientific American*, 217 (1967): 103–10. The original

passage appeared in James Clerk Maxwell, *Theory of Heat* (London: Longmans, Green, 1871), p. 328.

19. Leon Brillouin, "Maxwell's Demon Cannot Operate: Information and Entropy, I and II," *Journal of Applied Physics* 22 (1951): 334–43. Brillouin elaborated on his dispute with Shannon in the opening chapter of *Science and Information Theory* (New York: Academic Press, 1956). Shannon's papers are reprinted with a commentary by Warren Weaver in Shannon and Weaver, *The Mathematical Theory of Communication* (Urbana: University of Illinois Press, 1949).

20. For a discussion of this debate (a controversy that, itself, was not innocent of metaphors), see my "Self-Reflexive Metaphors in Maxwell's Demon and Shannon's Choice: Finding the Passages," in *Literature and Science: Theory and Practice,* ed. Stuart Peterfreund (Boston: Northeastern University Press, 1990). Palmeri in "Neither Literally Nor As Metaphor," relying primarily on the work of Edwin Jaynes in *The Maximum Entropy Formulation,* ed. Myron Tribus and Raphael Levine (Cambridge: MIT Press, 1979), argues that subsequent events proved Brillouin right, Shannon wrong. Jaynes is a prominent physicist who has published ground-breaking work on the connection between statistical mechanics and thermodynamic entropy; his views are not to be taken lightly. Nevertheless, the assertion that Shannon is simply wrong is misleading. Shannon's convention is still standard in electrical engineering, as a survey of twenty-seven textbooks shows (see Hayles, "Self-Reflexive Metaphors"). Moreover, Shannon's formulation has strong connections with the work of Ilya Prigogine and others in irreversible thermodynamics. From the viewpoint of chaos theory, Shannon's formulation is more productive than Brillouin's. For another view than Jaynes's, see Henri Atlan, "On a Formal Definition of Organization," *Journal of Theoretical Biology* 45 (1974): 295–304. For a fuller discussion of this entire issue, see my *Chaos Bound: Orderly Disorder in Contemporary Literature and Science* (Ithaca: Cornell University Press, 1990).

21. Ilya Prigogine and Isabelle Stengers summarize much of this work in *Order Out of Chaos: Man's New Dialogue with Nature* (New York: Bantam, 1984).

22. Edgard Gunzig, Jules Geheniau, and Ilya Prigogine, "Entropy and Cosmology," *Nature* 330 (1987): 621–4.

23. Thomas Pynchon in the "Introduction" to *Slow Learner: Early Stories* (Boston: Little, Brown, 1984) warns the reader not to underestimate his ignorance of entropy and other scientific concepts, or the shallowness with which he uses them in his work (pp. 14–15). Yet even

as he denies any profound understanding of entropy, his comments reveal that he knows at least as much as I have summarized here. For a discussion of Pynchon's story "Entropy," see David Seed, "Order in Thomas Pynchon's 'Entropy,' " in Bloom, ed. *Thomas Pynchon: Modern Critical Views,* pp. 157–74.

24. The significance of the agriculture/technology crossing has been noticed by Thomas Hill Schaub, "Open Letter in Response to Edward Mendelson's 'The Sacred, the Profane, and *The Crying of Lot 49,* ' " *boundary 2* (1976): 93–101.

25. That language does not fall short of ultimate revelation, in *The Crying of Lot 49* and other works by Pynchon, is the point of Molly Hite's " 'Holy-Center Approaching' in the Novels of Thomas Pynchon," *Journal of Narrative Technique* 12 (1982): 121–9.

26. The Puritan connection, implicit here, is brought into strong relief in *Gravity's Rainbow,* as is the denial of the human reality of death, discussed later in this essay.

27. The necessity for balance is the point of Schaub's "Open Letter." Schaub is concerned that Mendelson, in emphasizing the text's hierophanies, may make the novel more revelatory and less ambiguous than it really is.

28. This change in the Tristero is discussed by Eric White in "Negentropy, Noise, and Emancipatory Thought," *Chaos and Order: Complex Dynamics in Literature and Science,* ed. N. Katherine Hayles (Chicago: University of Chicago Press, 1991).

29. This concern surfaces in a different way in Pynchon's "Introduction" to *Slow Learner,* where he finds his early work lacking because it began from abstract concepts rather than from a strong sense of character.

30. Mendelson, "The Sacred, the Profane, and *The Crying of Lot 49.*"

A Re-cognition of Her Errand into the Wilderness

PIERRE-YVES PETILLON

> In the meantime, in between time . . .
> — Popular song

> Where have you been in the uterim?
> — *Finnegans Wake*

IT is, to use a highly typical Pynchon word, rather "odd" that *The Crying of Lot 49*, a slim novella which, because he was short of cash, Thomas Pynchon dashed off for *Esquire* on time borrowed from a long haul of erecting the vast cathedral of *Gravity's Rainbow*, should have become an overnight classic. *The Crying of Lot 49* remains, arguably, the most emblematic text of the American sixties, and one that, a quarter-century later, has best retained its magical spell over the reader.[1] When this fictional UFO first fell from the strange skies of America, the effect, at least on the European side of the Atlantic, was definitely eerie and even downright (as we had not yet learned to say) "mind-boggling." The few of us who had been there at all saw it as nothing more than a hilarious "black humor" cartoon of the current southern California's "freaked-out" scene. Some already knew about the Tibetan *Book of the Dead*, having read *The Psychedelic Experience* two years before and noticing Dr. Hilarius was obviously Timothy Leary scarcely transmogrified.[2] This was the year when Dr. Leary, spurred on by Marshall McLuhan, coined his slogan "Turn On, Tune In, Drop Out" – and at the time this seemed a fairly adequate summary of the story told in *The Crying of Lot 49*.[3] That seemed to settle it, then: from the same people who brought you the Merry Pranksters and the Hell's Angels, the Grateful Dead and Ravi Shankar, here was another "groovy" sample of the emergent psychedelic scene: Om,

Sweet Om, O(edipa) M(aas) and her Lonely Hearts Club Band.[4] Except that some of us – and there were many for whom "L.S.D." meant "pound, shillings and pence," who had been brought up on *The Waste Land* and *Four Quartets,* and for whom T. S. Eliot had become something like a native language – were puzzled and slightly disturbed that the novel should be fraught with so many half-buried quotations and echoes of our cultural hero. How did this square with the novel's zany humor, and how had it come about that the Archbishop of Canterbury (who had just died the year before, and was still being mourned) had thus gotten posthumously stranded, as it were, on Laguna Beach? Others were fascinated by the formal intricacies of this sophisticated Borges-like artifact. One was on more familiar ground here, having read if not "Osberg," then at least Nabokov's *Pale Fire.*[5] Although the tonality and mood of Pynchon's novel were hard to place, the book was obviously part of the experimental trend in literature spurred by the example of the Russian wordsmith and magician.

In some ways, a French reader felt almost at home in *The Crying of Lot 49,* as the novel clearly had some sort of kinship with the fancy tricks the Raymond Queneau–George Perec–Harry Matthews–Italo Calvino crowd (the OULIPO Workshop of Potential Literature founded in 1960) was already up to on the Continent. Harry Matthews was living in Paris then, and *The Conversions,* published in 1962, had already told a story that, four years later, Oedipa's seemed almost to duplicate. In Matthews's novel, as well, there is a wealthy eccentric who leaves behind a cryptic will which the would-be heir to the estate has to decipher, puzzling out riddles, scrutinizing texts and hunting for clues, eventually stumbling upon a secret society which has survived persecution through several centuries by going underground.[6] The hero of *The Conversions* is equally caught up in a "conspiracy" and wonders whether the secret society might not be the shadow-image of the estate itself, occasionally suspecting along the way that the whole plot might have been devised by some wily mastermind just to lure him into some sort of hermeneutic fool's errand. Furthermore, Matthews' novel strongly suggests, as does Pynchon's, that the protagonist's fate inside the story is but a mirror-image of the reader's predicament as he (or she) works his (or her) way through the novel's labyrinths – that the novel inculcates a self-reflexive game played through the process of reading itself.

The Crying of Lot 49 was thus, from one perspective, read and deciphered as just another fantastic brain-teaser. And yet, without being unduly harsh to Matthews, whose book remains a delight to read, one rapidly comes to feel that the two novels are worlds apart. For the odd thing about Pynchon's novel is that even when the reader has "puzzled it out," once the game is up, the particular spell of the work does not vanish. Its "mood," if anything, grows upon you with each rereading. After a quarter-century spent tracking clues and sources, the novella should be dead by now, crushed under a scholastic gravestone. Logically, it should not be breathing any more; but breathe it still does.

I would submit that the magical spell exerted by *The Crying of Lot 49* is due not to the Borges-like intricacies of its craft as such, but to its "topicality." By this, I do not so much refer to topical references, though they are there (the aforementioned Timothy Leary, Goldwater's 1964 presidential campaign, Stockhausen's music, the Beatles), but to a more unobtrusive kind of topicality. *The Crying of Lot 49* captures the particular "mood" of the times; it conjures up the "time-ghost" (Pynchon's own translation of the German *Zeitgeist*) as few works of fiction manage to do. It thus belongs in a class which would include *The Catcher in the Rye* for the fifties, *Dangling Man* for the forties, and *The Great Gatsby* for the twenties. The achievement is all the more impressive because the mood it captures is slightly off-key, the mood of an "awkward" transition between two epochs, a transitional period. *The Crying of Lot 49* is not a novel of the sixties as, say, Ken Kesey's *One Flew Over the Cuckoo's Nest* is a novel of 1960–62, or Richard Brautigan's *Trout Fishing in America* is a novel of 1963, or Philip Roth's *Portnoy's Complaint* is a novel of 1966–69. The story admittedly does take place in the summer of 1964, and partly, at least, on the Berkeley campus, where a puzzled Oedipa ventures and sees a "riot" about to explode, but it is in no way "a novel of 1964"; rather, it is a novel moving from 1957 to 1964 which portrays how it felt to live through that period of "transition," a novel about those seven years spent brooding and "waiting" for the new times to be born.[7]

To make sense of that topicality, it seems preferable to refer

Pynchon's novel back to Kerouac's *On the Road* than to the kinds of technical experimentation practiced by Borges, Nabokov, or the OULIPO group. The novel's topicality, its sense of transition, is conveyed by the very *structure* of the book, thus transforming it into an artifact or icon of the times. But this structure is in turn made to mirror, slyly and self-consciously, the entire "great tradition" of American fiction. One way of reading *The Crying of Lot 49* is to see the novel as a sort of textual black hole into which the whole of American fiction could somehow collapse, or conversely, as a white hole out of which, should one run the movie backward, it can be viewed retrospectively being born. That smooth transition from the topical to the structural to the historical is, I will argue, the outstanding feature of the work, while its main achievement is that the voice one hears throughout – Pynchon's voice – with its unmistakable stamp, should survive this exercise in iconic archaeology or ethnography and retain to the end, and past the end, its lyrical thrust and particular vibrato.

"Humming out there"

Everything, in a way, started with Kerouac. *The Crying of Lot 49* is haunted by scattered reminiscences of Kerouac's *On the Road.* Both works convey the sense of a world "blooming," as if awakening from a long sleep. Very much like Kerouac's, Oedipa's experience is one of moving "across the tracks" toward an invisible, hidden America: a sad world of "shacks and rags" whose peculiar note of "tristessa" (to quote the title of another Kerouac book) is echoed in the Tristero. Largely from Kerouac as well (one feels) is derived the sense that as one crosses over to the other side of the tracks, one falls out of the official grid superimposed on the land and into a sort of twilight zone (what William Burroughs calls the Interzone) where, emerging from time into "timeless shadows," one becomes a "ghost." Kerouac's "beat time" in San Francisco, where he walks around picking up butts from the street and, with Marylou, visits "some drunken seaman in a flophouse on Mission Street," more than foreshadows Oedipa's experience in the Embarcadero when, like a mourning Pietà, she nurses a dying sailor. In *On the Road,* moving across the tracks revives voices long past and forgotten, drifting from industrial Lowell where Kerouac's childhood was spent: "Voices of old companions and brothers under the bridge, among the motorcycles, along the washlined neighborhood and drowsy doorsteps of an afternoon, where boys played guitars while their older brothers worked in the mills."[8] Similarly, Oedipa, as she ventures deeper into Tristero territory, increasingly feels she is "meant to remember" and to redeem from near-oblivion voices that without her would fade past the threshold of consciousness and be lost forever. Although Pynchon will mainly construe his concept of "waste" through Eliot's *The Waste Land*, the sense of becoming part of the "waste" is evoked throughout Kerouac's novel, climaxing in the chapter where Sal Paradise falls asleep in an all-night movie on Detroit's skid row, and at dawn, "embryonically convoluted among the rubbish," is nearly swept up with "the come and gone" as part of the waste. Finally, *On the Road* contains the eschatological suggestion that, hidden, invisible, in the shadows across the tracks, a whole "silent empire," that of the "fellahin," the "people of the earth" Kerouac read about in Spengler, are waiting for their Kingdom to come. They are as yet still below the threshold of speech, but their "mournful wail" will one day prevail. They are those who both "walk in darkness" and "wait in darkness."[9] And their motto could already be: "We Await Silent Tristero's Empire."

The mood of *The Crying of Lot 49* is so close to that of Kerouac's beat novel that one could easily unearth further echoes and reminiscences, but more crucial is the fact that Pynchon's central icon, the Tristero "horn," should derive from the "horn" or saxophone that one hears blowing throughout Kerouac's novel, from the "little Harlem" of Folsom Street in San Francisco, where the black musician "hopped and monkeydanced with his magic horn and blew hundred choruses of blues" (190), to Detroit, where the blues on the horn, in the wild bop night, is perceived by Kerouac as the first intimation of the "last tune," as "every now and then a clear harmonic cry gave new suggestions of a tune that would someday be the only tune in the world and would raise men's souls to joy" (228). Now, there are several critical differences between the Kerouac "horn" of 1951–57 and Pynchon's of 1964–66, some of them obliquely reflecting the drift of American culture through those years. First, in keeping with the new linguistic self-consciousness exhibited by the American novel, the "horn" in Pynchon has become an icon (a scriptural graffito on the wall) and a word woven into the warp and woof of lexical memory – in both cases, a cryptic sign to be detected and deciphered. Second, the word turns out to be a key-word which, as the story unfolds, will unlock stratum after stratum of buried historical material. A third difference which conveys the "topical" quality of the novel is that Pynchon's horn has become muted: muted, "as so many things in those days," Pynchon adds, referring to the climate of the fifties.[10]

In the late fifties, when he was about twenty and starting to write, Pynchon appears to have been more drawn to the ecstatic "howl" or "whoopee" of the Beats than to the low-profile, sullen, sulking figure of the "hipster" – and "muted" is a word that does crop up fairly often in those days to describe that cultural figure. Thus, in a 1957 *Harper's Bazaar* article that Norman Mailer drew upon for his depiction of the "White Negro," the hipster is said to have "that muted animal voice which shivered the national attention when first used by Marlon Brando," and to "come out of the muted rebellion of the proletariat."[11] In *The Crying of Lot 49,* the "muted horn" becomes an emblem of the whole "silent generation" which came of age in the fifties – a generation kept in check, sexually and otherwise, as the sly, silent pun on "horn/horny" suggests.[12] By 1957, sensitive observers felt that a (still "muted") rebellion was underway; seven years later, it exploded in the raucous "riots" at Berkeley. Those seven years that saw the shift from silence to outcry, or at least to the threshold of outcry, are the hidden background, and indeed the very theme, of Pynchon's novel.

Whereas Kerouac and his crowd crisscrossing the continent felt they were living in the eye of the whirlwind, catching ecstatically what they called "It," Pynchon's keynote is that everything comes through muffled, as if registered from afar. As Pynchon explains, when the Beat generation first burst on the scene in 1955–57, he was at Cornell, living within walls – walled in, as it were, in a self-enclosed tower – but "thanks to all those alternative low-life data that kept filtering insidiously through the ivy, we had begun to get a sense of that other world humming out there."[13] *The Crying of Lot*

49 is a Beat novel, the last of the Beat novels – call it a post-Beat novel – but one in which the typical Beat experience looms up slowly into view, as if through a glass darkly, or picked up as a faraway sound. The main emphasis is on the medium through which "it" registers. This characteristic Pynchonian stance is probably best captured in his short story "The Secret Integration" about a black jazz musician named McAfee. McAfee has been "on the road," but the story is told through the consciousness of a young boy who has never left his small town, snugly ensconced in Hawthorne's Berkshires: "It was as if Mr. McAfee . . . was broadcasting from somewhere quite distant, telling about things Tim would not be sure of in the daylight."[14] There is another world "out there," a shadowy world broadcasting at night on the lower frequencies tuned in secretly. When McAfee calls the West Coast on the telephone, young Tim listens "while more clicks and whirs went out like hard fingers, going across the whole country in he dark trying to touch one person out of all the millions that lived in it" (183). Similarly, at the end of *The Crying of Lot 49*, Oedipa will tune in to what will have in the meantime become a whole chorus of silent voices. When is a "hum" more than a hum? When it is so "muffled" as to come close to silence, or when this silence is so deep as to be almost a cry? Such questions are echoed and amplified in *The Crying of Lot 49*.

In some sense, it could be argued that the whole story of *The Crying of Lot 49* could be seen in embryo – "embryonically convoluted," as it were – in a single episode of Ralph Ellison's *Invisible Man*. The episode occurs just after Clifton Todd's death, when the protagonist in a Harlem subway station wonders why his friend chose "to plunge into nothingness, into the voice of faceless faces, of soundless voices, lying outside history." Suddenly spotting a group of black youths in zoot suits he would not have noticed before, he proclaims:

> What about those fellows *waiting* still and *silent* there on the platform, so still and silent that they clash with the crowd in their very immobility; standing *noisy* in their very *silence;* harsh as a *cry* of *terror* in their quietness? . . . Everyone must have seen them, or heard their *muted* laughter . . . or perhaps failed to see them at all. For they were men outside of historical time . . .[15]

Waiting, silence, noise, muted, cry, terror: the basic lexicon of *The Crying of Lot 49* is there. The way, even, "they seem to move like dancers in some kind of funeral ceremony, swaying, going forward, their black faces secret, moving slowly down the subway platform" (440) seems to foreshadow the black-clad dancers of, presumably, the Tristero. "They were outside the groove of history" (444). At this point Ellison's protagonist, as a member of the Brotherhood (the Communist Party), or so he fancies himself, is still very much inside the groove of history. But the suspicion starts gnawing at him that "the languid blues" he hears, reminiscent of "down South," might be all that will finally be "recorded" – "the only true history of the times" – and he starts tuning in that other frequency, becoming the man who asks at the end of the novel: "who knows but that, on the lower frequencies, I speak for you?" (581). In a similar fashion, Oedipa Maas gradually becomes what Pynchon in *Gravity's Rainbow* will portray as "a lower-frequency listener," opening up her spectrum to the hum out there, half-silence, half-noise, from which, as a medium of informational exchange, she will extract voices and, ultimately, a cry.[16]

Betwixt & Between

Ellison's Harlem zoot-suiters are "men of transition," neither here nor there, belonging, in the Harlem phrase, "nowhere." They speak "a jived-up transitional language full of country glamour, think transitional thought" (441). They are transitional, first, in the sociological sense (they are halfway between their rural deep South and the new stage of historical consciousness Ellison's protagonist still thinks, at this point, he represents), but in a more radical sense as well: "they are men out of time, who would soon be gone and forgotten," the last remnants of a vanishing America slowly dwindling toward extinction (441). Although they still dream the old ancient dreams, they are almost ghosts, almost "disappeared." And yet (the Invisible Man wonders), "who knew but they were saviors, the true leaders, the bearers of something precious?" (441). This renders them "transitional" in the sense of ushering in a new world: not a world about to vanish but one about to be born. Ellison's reversal from ghostly extinction to eschatological expectation (which can be traced back to Eliot) is key to Pynchon's construction of his own "topical" sense of belonging to a transitional generation – in T. S. Eliot's phrase, "torn on the horn between season and season."[17] Pynchon came of age during "the Eisenhower siesta," when everything had, it seemed, slowed to a standstill, giving that sense of utter stasis Holden Caulfield, walking through Central Park on a "lousy" Sunday, had so memorably described: "It didn't seem at all like Christmas was coming soon. It didn't seem like anything was coming."[18] This came to an abrupt end in 1957 when America was jolted out of its complacency by the shattering news that the Russian *Sputnik* was orbiting the earth, and started waking from its drowsy, almost Edwardian languor. *The Crying of Lot 49* is a record of that slow process of awakening, as new voices "humming out there," at first muffled and faintly heard, began to register.

Pynchon's achievement is not just that he is able to suggest, atmospherically as it were, the topical mood of those "in-between" times, the sense of being between two worlds, but that he has managed to build that thematic "in-betweenness" into the very structure of his work. This he achieves by using the basic concepts of information theory.[19] As early as 1959, in the short story "Entropy," Pynchon had mapped out his – but also his times' – epistemological space in which he imagined a two-story house in Washington. Upstairs, an enclosure, hermetically sealed, with its occupant practicing a policy of "containment" (as it was called in those days), trying to protect his enclave from outside invasion and to keep his signal free of any parasitic noise. Downstairs, a room wide open, with people walking in and out, speaking in a pentecostal babel of voices rising, in a sexual crescendo, towards "riot." In information theory, the unit of information is the binary digit or "bit" which "communicates" a choice between two equally probable messages. The switch is either "on" or "off"; one sends either an electrical impulse, or no impulse. Onto that stark binary concept (1/0) Pynchon will gradually come to graft a whole symbolic structure where 1/0 (one/zero) could be better read as I/O (on/off).[20] Upstairs is pole I: the channel through which the message is perceived is so narrow as to filter out all "noise"; what one registers is perfectly patterned and ordered so that nothing unexpected or unpredictable comes through; all is redundancy. Downstairs, one swings all the way across to pole O. There, total randomness reigns. Each instant something unpredictable, utterly original, is likely to happen. But here there is no pattern or repetition – no gestalt – to hold "reality" together in a recognizable shape; it therefore threatens to decay into chaos. Either order, but utterly predictable, or originality, but utterly random: these are the two epistemological limits negotiated in "Entropy" and in Pynchon's fiction at large.

In a way, this epistemological dichotomy could be read as a topographical survey of the literary landscape of the fifties. Although novels like Saul Bellow's *The Victim* or, again, Ellison's *Invisible Man* provide apt illustrations, perhaps this topography shows best in the field of poetry. On the one hand, readers were under the thrall of the self-enclosed form inherited from the New Criticism, the poetic icon such as one finds in, for example, Richard Wilbur or the early Adrienne Rich. There was, "in those days," a cult of self-insulation (what Oedipa calls her "encapsulation in the tower") where order is indeed achieved within the poem, but as a bulwark against the threat of disorder, as a shelter against the "terror outside": one would, figuratively, fasten the shutters and safely retreat into a tightly sealed enclosure. But the schizophrenic fifties were also the time of – as exemplified in the work of John Cage or the Black Mountain poets – a countermovement in quest of an "opening of the field," a poetics of exposure (occasionally of self-exposure) to the randomness "out there."

Pynchon neatly registers this tension in the range of his work. From Meatball Mulligan in "Entropy" to Roger Mexico in *Gravity's Rainbow,* the key character in his novels and stories is the man or woman on the borderline between the I and O, halfway between closure and openness. In "Entropy," despite Meatball's movement to and fro across the border, the sketched diagram remains fairly static. Similarly, from a structural point of view, in *V.* the narrative is (as the title graphically implies) split in the middle. One branch focuses on Stencil the decipherer, alert to "signs and symptoms" appearing "up there," searching for the sacred and secret pattern behind appearances, waiting for an awful, ultimate revelation. The other follows Profane, the schlemiel, as he drifts randomly and goes "downward" in the randy way of all flesh. To find a dynamic scheme, one has to go to another early story, "The Small Rain," where the main character, dropping out of the official grid and lapsing back into sleep, withdraws from the Republic and then discovers the unsuspected spectrum "beyond the ultra-violet and the infra-red" as he becomes aware of other, unheard voices.

In *The Crying of Lot 49* one finds for the first time both the map (enclosure vs. the wilderness, or chaos) and the dynamic scheme as the two branches of *V.* are fused into one story. Oedipa Maas, as her name implies, is both a decipherer and a drifter. As "Oedipa" she tries to solve riddles as she follows the rainbow of "God's plot" across the sky. As "Maas," she is what in Newtonian times was called a "masse grave," feeling the downward pull of gravity and going "the way of all flesh," heavy ("gravis") in more ways than one.[21] Transitional Oedipa moves from the "I" of decipherment and self-enclosure to the "O" of randomness, the key moment in her voyage being the "nighttown" chapter in San Francisco where she starts to "drift . . . at random, and watch nothing happen" (109). As she travels – and American culture from 1957 to 1964 along with her – she goes through a period of "anomie." The homeostatic state she used to live in has broken down: her enclosure has been "pierced" open; she now passes from one state to the threshold of another. Just as in what anthropologists, after Van Gennep, call a "rite of passage," she finds herself in a liminal state. She is a "passenger," and her nighttime journey leads her into the ghostly world of a no-man's-land, an in-between twilight zone whose inhabitants are either half-dead or still to be born.

The "whole story" of the novel takes place in an interim period of 49 days, a time which can be construed in two ways. First, 49 is 50 minus one, the fiftieth day of the Christian liturgical calendar (after Easter) being the Pentecost. The story takes place in the 49 days between the Easter rising of Christ and the awaited Pentecost when the Holy Ghost, speaking in a babble of voices, will typologically foreshadow the Day of Doom and ultimate revelation. But the 49 days also refers to another "interim," the 49 days during which, in the Tibetan *Book of the Dead,* the newly deceased slowly work their way toward final death and rest. In this sense, the interim period points not only forward to the "awful" things to come, but also backward toward a world slowly dwindling into oblivion.[22] This interim is, in classic typological fashion, a link between memory and prophecy; thus, Oedipa, standing at the interface between the two kingdoms of legacy and prophecy, is kept simultaneously remembering and expecting. As described by Van Gennep, a "rite of passage" normally falls into three stages: first, separation from the old order; then the "interim," the liminal or threshold period itself; and finally reintegration into the new order.[23] But in *The Crying of Lot 49*, the whole emphasis is on the interim period, and the story stops abruptly just as the passenger is about to enter a radically new order, when the auctioneer, whose name is "Passerine," is about to "pass'er in" to the Other Kingdom.[24] In *Gravity's Rainbow*, Slothrop will move all the way from enclosure to exposure, from the scrutiny of signs "up there" to the fall into a carnival of flesh. In light of the American tradition, what makes Oedipa's story more subtly significant is that she remains on the threshold. She recapitulates the American experience of moving beyond the "hedge" to the "edge." Having started in a hedged-in enclosure, she eventually comes "to an edge," both of space (the edge of the Pacific, "the hole left by the moon tearing free and monument to her exile") and, as we shall see, of time. That threshold, in an Orphic reading of the book, is the pierced interface between the two kingdoms, but located in what has been from Thoreau through Frederick Jackson Turner the American "site" or locus par excellence.[25] Like Thoreau, Oedipa is a "borderer," and her westering impulse takes her to the "edge" of her clearing, where the foreign "out there" begins. She stands on a "borderline invisible, but felt at its crossing, between worlds" – from way back, a most (perhaps *the* most) "typical" American locus.[26]

Loomings

Reference to a "new-fangled" information theory or to the latest technological devices through which, in Pynchon, the "other" world registers cannot conceal how basically Jamesian, in its general drift, is the story told in *The Crying of Lot 49*. Like so many of James's characters (Isabel Archer, Lambert Strether, Milly Theale), "Young Republican" Oedipa Maas is dislodged from a static, timeless isolation (something like a New England enclosure of the mind) and slowly lured into the open to wander and get lost in a labyrinth of signs she is meant to decipher. Admittedly, one is unlikely to find in genteel Henry James obscene graffiti scrawled on toilet stalls (save by innuendo), but Oedipa nevertheless undergoes the typically Jamesian ordeal of being swamped by clues registering subliminally on her consciousness. She is James's "candid outsider," suddenly exposed to the intimacy of "another world," the "innocent eye" whose plight, in Tony Tanner's phrase, is "not so much its horror at what it sees, as its bewilderment at what it only half sees."[27] Oedipa's story is first and foremost the record of her epistemological bewilderment. Her work is to sift and sort through half-glimpsed signs and clues, to piece together scattered fragments so that, finally, everything can fit together in "clear plot" which comes to be named Tristero. But just as with James, Oedipa is never sure whether the plot is indeed a hidden order she has actually detected and deciphered; or a hoax which has been played on her, with someone mischievously and purposefully planting clues; or her own mental construction, something which, in her desperate attempt to find a key to it all, she has been hallucinating all along. Whatever the case, the whole drama of epistemological uncertainty takes place (a further Jamesian feature) in her own consciousness. Everything looms, as through a glass darkly, through the medium of that consciousness; throughout the novel, the reader has the highly Jamesian sense of Oedipa watching the screen of her own consciousness where things register whose significance only appears "afterwards." "She was afterwards to recall," "it was one of the things she afterwards saw," "a small grave intimation, something into which he afterwards read the meaning" – every reader of James knows how often such phrases recur.[28] Similarly, there is no real unmediated present in *The Crying of Lot 49;* the story told is not what happens to Oedipa, but her slow recognition that something has already happened somewhere in a shadowy past and her expectation of what, once it is wholly deciphered and "blooms" for her in full consciousness, it will foreshadow for the future.

In his quarrel with Edgar Allan Poe, James insisted that "the fantastic" should loom through "a most ordinary consciousness."[29]

As an Orange County Republican housewife locked in the most trivial suburban routine, circumscribed by her narrow education in the smug fifties, Oedipa has, at least at the outset, a consciousness as "ordinary" as they come. But once she has been "pierced," her consciousness becomes just that "pierced aperture" (James's phrase) through which an increasingly fantastic, perhaps phantasmic landscape is perceived.[30] Indeed, the Tristero underground, the hidden empire of disinheritance Oedipa stumbles upon (or so it seems) is highly reminiscent of the London anarchist underground James described in *his* novel about the disinherited, *The Princess Casamassima;* and Pynchon's technique for presenting it follows, in broad outline, James's rule: "My scheme called for the suggested nearness (to all our apparently ordered life) of some sinister anarchic underworld, heaving in its pain, its power and its hate: a presentation, not of sharp particulars, but of loose appearances, vague motions and sounds and symptoms, just perceptible presences and general looming possibilities."[31] As Oedipa steps across the tracks and into a territory lying both beyond and beneath the official grid, the "effects" produced on her as well as on the reader are just those James claimed he was working for, "precisely those of our not knowing, of society's not knowing, but only guessing and suspecting and trying to ignore what 'goes on' irreconcilably, subversively, beneath the vast smug surface."[32]

Finally – perhaps the most significantly Jamesian feature of all – *The Crying of Lot 49* not only focuses on Oedipa's epistemological bewilderment, but also charts the gradual "opening out" of her field of awareness. Her foray into the land of the Tristero, with its Catholic, European, and imperial overtones, is similar to Lambert Strether's own venture into a dark foreign territory where, dislocated from his native (highly Republican and Puritan) Woolett, he finds himself in Paris, drifting into that "far-off hum," into the world "humming out there" that will gradually overwhelm him: "Nothing could be odder than Strether's sense of himself at that moment, launched into something of which the sense would be quite disconnected from the sense of his past and which was literally beginning there and then."[33] Something "odd" happens to him, just as something "odd" happens to "Oed" – the fond nickname her husband gives her. "OED" is, among other things, the abbreviation for the *Oxford English Dictionary*, as befits a character so "hung up on words"; but "odd" is also there, a buried echo. "Odd" is also a favorite word of James's, who submits it to all sorts of grammatical twists.[34] But close scrutiny of *The Crying of Lot 49* would show how often it crops up there as well: at the beginning, having received a mysterious "call," Oedipa is seen "shuffling back through a fat deckful of days" to find out whether they are all identical "or pointing the same way subtly like a conjurer's deck, any odd one readily clear to the trained eye" (11); and then there are these – "'Then give me the odds'" (34); "Oddly, the preface was unsigned" (90); "Odds are the author will be dead" (93); or "'Odd,' Cohen agreed. 'The transposition . . . is only on the Lincoln 4¢'" (98). But then, texts are made up of words, and there would be little justification in singling out "odd" and making it the "odd word out" if a passage in *Gravity's Rainbow* did not underlie how odd, as a word, "odd" is. Statistician Roger Mexico – another borderer of sorts – is discussing a phenomenon which he describes as a "statistical oddity." He then adds: "'Odd, odd, odd, think of the word: such white finality in the closing clap of the tongue. It implies moving past the tongue-stop – beyond the zero – and into the other realm. Of course you don't move past. But you realize, intellectually, that's how you *ought* to be moving.'"[35]

"Odd," then, is the signal that one is about to move past the threshold into uncharted territory. When Oedipa has her first near-hierophany with a "revelation" trembling "just past the threshold of her understanding," "she and the Chevy seemed parked at the centre of an odd, religious instant. As if, on some other frequency, or out of the eye of some whirlwind rotating too slow for her heated skin even to feel the centrifugal coolness of, words were being spoken. She suspected that much" (24–5). The instant is not odd because religious, but religious because odd. Just as Strether "felt (again) the brush of his senses of moving in a maze of mystic, closed allusions," Oedipa finds herself roaming among signs all pointing to the Tristero. Strether attempts to see "how it all fitted, yet there seemed one loose piece" which "little by little looms up," until he has the revelation that is "the deep, deep truth of intimacy revealed."[36] Like Strether, Oedipa finds herself peeping into a forbidden world, utterly alien to her experience, and "in contact with that element as [she] has never so intimately been," she, like Strether, "[has] the consciousness of opening to it, for the happy instant, all the windows of [her] mind, of letting this rather gray interior drink in for once the sun of a climate not marked in [her] old geography" – in her case, the "black sun of melancholia," a shadow-sun, as it were.[37] The two novels record similar processes of vision through which a hidden and forbidden world looms up until one comes to the threshold of a "flash" – another key word for both authors – a "spasm of consciousness" (James's phrase) experienced when one is exposed to utter "otherness."[38] As Strether experiences it in Gloriani's garden, the "flash" is both glorious revelation and tigerish terror. In this gradual "opening of the field" we note what one might call the Emersonian edge of the looming process where exposure edges into overexposure, and revelation floods the consciousness, "leaving an overexposed blank when the ordinary world came back" (95). This process in Pynchon reflects the interface between modern consciousness and technology – the movie screen (as when Oedipa feels she is "watching a movie just perceptibly out of focus, that the projectionist refuses to fix"), or the photographic plate (where "revelation" is the chemical process that brings the hidden image into view), or, as in *Vineland,* the television or computer screen (where the image "pixledances" into view) – but, in its general drift, Pynchon's is basically a reenactment of James's process of enlightenment.[39] There are two qualifications, however, which will be explored further. First, Pynchon's emphasis falls not on the slow process as such, but on the last moment, just before the threshold or moment of revelation. Second, as previously noted, in Pynchon's work one can hardly tell whether the image looms up into view (all the way to the edge of "revelation") from the depths of a ghostly past – as an aftershadow of things gone – or from an apocalyptic future rushing in, a foreshadowing of things to come.

Into, and out of, the scribble

Things gradually become "curiouser and curiouser" for Oedipa as she falls down the rabbit hole into an alternative world. Hers, though, is primarily a textual rabbit hole and she is lured into it, in the first place, through her close scrutiny of words – ultimately, perhaps, of the Word. Investigating the Inverarity estate involves learning intimately "the books," deciphering the will and testament the old man left behind after vanishing behind his grin like an absconded Cheshire Cat. She is faced with a scrambled text – a scribble – with all kinds of misprints, lacunae, and distortions, open to all kinds of misprisions. But her background has doubly trained Oedipa in textual exegesis. What makes her "just a whiz at pursuing strange words in Jacobean texts" (104) is both her Puritan ancestry (she, too, belongs to a dynasty of "word-smitten Puritans" she would be able to trace, as does Tyrone Slothrop in *Gravity's Rainbow,* all the way back to the seventeenth-century Jacobean England her ancestors left to come to the Lord's Plantation in the New World) and her education in the fifties, the heyday of New Criticism, when close scrutiny of the text as a self-enclosed icon held sway under the aegis of T. S. Eliot, himself a major commentator upon Jacobean drama.[40] Oedipa probably never would have left her suburban enclosure had she not been lured out of it by words, which give her a linguistic, and hence seemingly familiar, track to follow.

In its "scribbled" or intertextual aspect, *The Crying of Lot 49* is one of the most deliberately "foregrounded" texts in American fiction since *Lolita* or *Pale Fire;* but it is slyly so. There is, clearly, the play within the play which constitutes the parody of *The Courier's Tragedy;* the verbal showmanship is obvious and the emphasis falls on the writer's performance; but on the whole, and despite other linguistic quirks such as the wild swinging of diction between the lowly colloquial and the highly scholarly (an old American routine), linguistic pyrotechnics are not as important as the weight of linguistic memory that each word, though perfectly "ordinary" the first time around, eventually comes to bear. This makes the reading of *The Crying of Lot 49* a very peculiar experience. "Things" here loom up, as previously noted, through the medium of a Jamesian consciousness, but that medium has become thoroughly linguistic: not a clear, or even opaque, windowpane, but (the times having moved from Emerson to Wittgenstein – unless it is back to Cotton Mather) stratum upon stratum of literary reminiscence, imprint, and trace. For example, Oedipa's discovery of the "disinherited" hearkens back to Kerouac's nostalgia for the Great Depression in *On the Road,* and further back, to Jack Conroy's novel of the thirties, *The Disinherited.* But the way that Oedipa comes around to this discovery and recognition is through a cryptic hieroglyph (the muted horn) and a puzzling word under whose spell she will fall: "Trystero. The world hung in the air as the act ended and all lights were for a moment cut; hung in the dark to puzzle Oedipa Maas, but not yet to exert the power over her it was to" (75). That "word" eventually points to a hidden plot, the underground world of the Tristero, whose constant theme is "disinheritance" and whose originator has styled himself as the "desheredado" (the disinherited) and "fashioned a livery of black for his followers" (160). Dispossessed, the Tristero lives in the shadows, its world revolving around another sun, the black sun of melancholy.

Whatever Pynchon's own experience of moving across the tracks into the world of the disinherited – vicariously, through reading Kerouac, or actually, in his journey to Watts,[41] the crucial thing, as far as the novel is concerned, is that the whole concept of the Tristero seems to derive linguistically from a reference in Eliot's *The Waste Land* to *"le Prince d'Aquitaine à la tour abolie"* (line 430). This line itself bears a cryptic reference to Gerald de Nerval's poem "El Deschidado," in which most of the major themes of the Tristero are sounded (the exile into a shadowy, marginal world; the former prince whose "tower" has been "abolished"; the "black sun of melancholia").[42] Nerval's poem, in turn, takes its title from the motto on the shield of the mysterious Disinherited Knight who turns up at the beginning of Walter Scott's *Ivanhoe* to fight in the lists, and who will eventually represent both the Saxons and the Jews evicted from their estates by Norman chivalry. This might well seem the sort of crazy hunt for idle sources and clues that any would-be scholar feels he or she might indulge in, were it not that Pynchon is perfectly aware of the implications of those half-hidden references woven both lexically and thematically into his "text" at large. *Gravity's Rainbow* will reveal how deeply interested in such "esoterica" Pynchon is: there the "tour abolie" of Nerval's poem – itself drawing on esoteric lore – will be seen not only as a symbol of disinheritance, but also as the tower in the Tarot pack, blown down by the Holy Ghost so that voices can be heard — surely, in retrospect, a theme relevant to *The Crying of Lot 49*. Similarly, Pynchon will later graft onto the theme of disinheritance further reminiscences, this time of his beloved Rilke in the seventh of *The Duino Elegies*, where in each period when the world mysteriously turns, or is turned upside down, there appear the disinherited, who no longer possess what once was, and who cannot yet possess what is to come — an apt description of the state of the disinherited in *The Crying of Lot 49*.[43] Here, a wealth of references are not yet fully exfoliated, as they will be in *Gravity's Rainbow*, but they exist, embryonically as it were, making this novella — an offshoot, one remembers, of the vaster novel — so cryptically teasing. In this sense, Pynchon himself, as well as his reader, is slowly building up a repertoire of half-buried quotations and intertexts where almost every word is found to be pregnant with scriptural memories and foreshadowings.

A similar case could be made for the many allusive words of *The Crying of Lot 49*. The "horn" may be Kerouac's saxophone blowing in the night, but it is also an icon from the archival past as it recapitulates the "horn" of the Thurn & Taxis carriers, blown so that the gates of cities would open when they rode in late at night with the mail. Those gates are very much like that "horn'd gate" of sleep "shadows" which the "real" world breaks through.[44] These are the gates dreams break through, or (as previously suggested) the "horn" "between season and season" upon which one is torn. In Eliot's *Little Gidding*, the world fades on the blowing of this horn, which would take us, along the typological track, all the way to the shofar of Doomsday.

This kind of textual compression makes reading *The Crying of Lot 49* a peculiar experience, closer in some respects to reading a contemporary poem by, say, Richard Wilbur, than to reading a "novel" in the usual sense. As the story unfolds, the reader is made increasingly "word-conscious" as each word becomes, figuratively, more conscious of both its etymological roots and its semantic field, so that eventually each word potentially suggests a whole knotty cluster of meanings: thus "ghost," or as previously noted, "odd." Or take "cry," which comes to mean (1) cry, as in tears — Oedipa crying for her beloved country, her forlorn America; (2) to cry as in the auction of the novel's title; (3) cry, as a voice crying in the wilderness preparing the way of the Lord, or the scriptural "cry at midnight" which, as in *Gravity's Rainbow*, the forever suspended "scream across the sky" ushers in at the end, "the cry which will abolish the night." There is the word "pierce" (Inverarity's first name, and the last name of the author of a major book on information theory) which implies both sexual violence (Metzger's and Oedipa's lovemaking reaches its climax as "his radiant eyes flew open, pierced her" [42]) and religious illumination ("a pure piercing grace note"), while the scriptural reminiscence of a "pierced" Jesus invites, again, a typological reading of the novel.[45] Just as, in the Old Testament, Eve was born from the "pierced" side of Adam, so in the New Testament the Church is born from the pierced side of Christ on the cross, and thus, in the new – and perhaps last – dispensation heralded by Pynchon's apocryphal gospel, from Oedipa's "pierced" bosom a new "invisible Church" is to be born. And there is "shadow," which first refers to Lamont Cranston, the Shadow of radio days, but eventually comes to mean (1) the ghostly double and alternative mirror-image of the world; and (2) as implied throughout, the "type" of foreshadowing of the world to come. And of course there is "deliver," which refers to (1) postal delivery of the mail; (2) deliverance, as the knight who delivers the maid imprisoned in her tower; (3) in many "deliverances" of seventeenth-century narratives of redemption from captivity; (4) redemption in general, as in Christ's deliverance of the redeemed; (5) delivery in the obstetrical sense, as Oedipa is both "pregnant" with meaning and delivered over to her fate in the end.[46] The list is endless, and this is precisely the point. The story seems to unfold along a horizontal axis, through time and space (or, more precisely, through an eschatological time-space), but as one reads, one recognizes what Pynchon, in another context, will call a "knotting into" of language.[47] Each of these (increasingly overdetermined) lexical knots threatens – as it slowly gathers a whole cluster of references – to stop the reading process altogether, or rather, to change it into something else, in which reading takes place no longer along the horizontal axis of the tale being told, but along a vertical, paradigmatic axis of decipherment. This experience is defined by Richard Brodhead for classic American fiction in a comparison he draws between nine-teenth-century American and British literature: the unfolding of the story through time and space (the journey or quest) suddenly stops short for a static moment – a "moment out of time," T. S. Eliot will call it – where one is called upon to watch and decipher a cryptic sign, whether the "awful hieroglyph" of *The Scarlet Letter* or the doubloon nailed to the *Pequod*'s mast.[48] One is led to sus-pect that what might look at first glance like postmodern self-reflexivity and linguistic self-consciousness in Pynchon might be more generally ascribed to a larger American legacy – that of the hieroglyph or emblem. The result is that *The Crying of Lot 49* is "pierced" with lexical "black holes" that threaten to swallow the tale altogether.

Indeed, the novel as a whole might be regarded as a "black hole" of sorts: like Borges, Pynchon is fascinated by "labyrinths, quibbles and emblems."[49] And yet, again as in Borges, what strikes the European reader is less the labyrinth itself than what it is ultimately erected to shelter us from: the awful and yet fascinat-ing vacancy outside. Whereas the world- and word-weary Euro-pean view reflected in Nabokov's work as well as Joyce's suggests that, deep as you may dig into the Ur-bog of the scribbled word, you will not find anything more than strata upon strata of age-old script, the main drift of Pynchon's work is to look for what Borges terms "The Other Tiger" – the tiger that, although inside language, would somehow jump out of it – and to move out of the scribbled enclosure into the "unscribbled territory."[50] In line with the Emer-sonian strain running through American literature, in *The Crying of Lot 49* there is a rock-bottom to be reached under the strata, a "blank" world somewhere beyond, or beneath, or before (and, consequently, after) the scribble one is deciphering.

In *Gravity's Rainbow*, Pynchon will list three ways of dealing with the text, or the "Ur-text," of the Rocket. Kabbalists look for the lost key of the text by scrambling the letters and, thus, puzzling out the scattered fragments in order to find a way back to the primeval root or word. Manicheans look for "another," shadowy text hidden under the official one. And Gnostics wait for the living voice to blow through the dead letter and burn it, so that the pristine voice can be heard anew. To some extent, all three approaches are reflected in *The Crying of Lot 49:* Oedipa is seen, in turn, puzzling out a scrambled testament, becoming aware of the Tristero as a shadowy double, and waiting for the "flash" of ultimate revelation. That is, Oedipa moves out of the enclosure of scribbled textual territory by moving beyond, before (and after), and below. Beyond, first, as she ventures to the edge of the Pacific, "the hole left free by the moon's tearing free and monument to her exile," and feels "somewhere beyond" some "unvoiced idea" lurking (55). Before (before, that is, the world was scattered into words, before the fall into language), as Oedipa wants to go back to the beginning when everything was still enclosed in some primeval fist and seen – in the blink of an eye – not in words but in signs "flashed for her on the sky." So it was, in the novel's rhetoric, at the beginning, and so it will be again when time comes to an end. But in the "meantime," where the novel takes place, what is most important is the sense of Oedipa's moving "below." There words yield to the silent world of the Tristero, and Oedipa, on her journey, listens to the almost silent "humming" of this world's motion, "the sounds of silence":[51]

> In the buses all night she listened to transistor radios playing songs in the lower stretches of the Top 200, that would never become popular, whose melodies and lyrics would perish as if they had never been sung. A Mexican girl, trying to hear one of these through snarling static from the bus's motor, hummed along as if she would remember it always, tracing post horns and hearts with a fingernail, in the haze of her breath on the window. (122)

The word "hum," as previously noted, is crucial here, and it is another of those Pynchonian words having a deep background in American literature. One remembers Whitman's "lullaby": "Not words, not music or rhyme I want, not custom or lecture, even the best / Only the lull I like, the hum of your valvèd voice."[52] The Tristero's "muted horn" is Pynchon's version of that "valvèd voice," but this goes a bit further than just reminiscence: as she listens in and eventually gives voice ("through me") to the "buried," "long-silent" voices, Oedipa alternately feels that these voices are either about to fade into subliminal silence and oblivion, or to explode into a wild pentecostal opera. Silent, blank wilderness, identity fading in empty space, or voices babbling in the wilderness – these have long been the two thresholds where American writers step out of the scribbled enclosure into another version, linguistic this time, of Wright Morris's "territory ahead." Wallace Stevens, in "An Ordinary Evening in New Haven," itself a quintessential recapitulation of the American vision, has memorably drawn the visual map of the place where this oscillation between thresholds takes place: from "naked Alpha," "the infant A standing on infant legs," to "hierophant Omega," "twisting, stooping, polymathic Z."[53] This oscillation is central to all of Pynchon's work, as *Gravity's Rainbow,* with its swing from the Dickinsonian "zero at the bone" to Borgesian illumination, will make clear. One version of this American trope is the embroidery masking the vacancy of the world, described at length in *V.* and hinted at in *The Crying of Lot 49.* In its primarily lyrical thrust, it is the vocal version of this trope (or, more precisely, topos, as it delineates an American space) which *The Crying of Lot 49,* better than any novel since World War Two, illustrates as it moves beyond the scribbled territory into something which is both naked silence and cry. In this space, both the world and the word, in a radical Protestant gesture, are swept clean of historical figurations to be, like the Trystero, "revealed in [their] terrible nakedness," but also as an operatic ejaculation of voices thus far unheard.

The "Other" America

As *The Crying of Lot 49* nears its end, the Tristero, which has been looming up all along, comes dangerously close to losing the teasing epistemological uncertainty it has retained thus far in the novel. As Oedipa stumbles along a railroad track, "over the cinderbed and its old sleepers," she remembers things she would have seen "if only she had looked" (179): squatters sleeping in freight cars or under canvas lean-tos stretched "behind smiling billboards along the highways" or "in junkyards in the stripped shells of wrecked Plymouths" (180). She discovers, in other words, an entire hobo jungle deeply hidden and seeming to have survived from the thirties. This finale has been pointed out by such critics as

Richard Poirier as a major flaw in the novel, an attempt through sheer rhetoric and lyrical oratory to express much more than the novel can carry in its "social" context.[54]

The Tristero underground has so far been implied to be a motley crew of eccentrics and bohemian drop-outs, an archipelago of "isolatoes" having "withdrawn" from the Republic, a lunatic fringe in tatters. But suddenly, in this last rhetorical leap, the Tristero broadens its scope to include, in a grand, almost liturgical gesture, all the outcasts of American history. One could agree (and this might be what Poirier finds questionable) that Pynchon, through his rhetoric, is trying to achieve in fiction what, he regrets, failed to happen in contemporaneous political life: the conjunction between "the Movement" (as represented by Students for a Democratic Society) and the "people."[55] By the end of the novel the Tristero, shadowy as it still remains, is no longer a ghostly underground (perhaps entirely phantasmatic) but a real, "embattled" underground about to come out of the shadows.[56] No longer hovering on the edge as a cryptic plot, the "Other" that the Tristero has thus far represented is almost revealed as a version of "the other America" that Michael Harrington described in a major book of the sixties whose "ghost" is very much felt in *The Crying of Lot 49*.[57] This America is "the America of poverty," "hidden today in a way it never was before," "dispossessed," "living on the fringes, the margin," as "internal exiles."[58]

Looking back at the novel from the perspective of its finale, it could almost be viewed as a New Deal novel, concerned with gathering back into the American fold a "third world" previously excluded. What would vanish in such a reading is the "other" side of the Tristero. For throughout the book the Tristero is "other" in another sense, carrying more "awful" implications: like the Lord, in the Calvinist view, it is perceived as "wholly other" (*totaliter aliter*), something human reason cannot possibly encompass, and whose advent – whose irruption into our world – would radically "turn it upside down," spelling terror as well as redemption as the two faces of its "awful" sovereignty. This twofold aspect of the Tristero in some ways reflects the twofold aspect of the Movement during the sixties.[59] Was the Movement an attempt to "turn the world upside down" and hasten – if need be, violently (like the

Anabaptists at Münster) – the Advent of the Kingdom, as those who subsequently drifted into the Weatherman terrorism seemed to think? Or was it, as Tom Hayden himself saw it, just an attempt to bring American back to herself and reawaken the old native heritage of the New Deal, and further back of the Wobblies?[60] Reading *Vineland* years later, one would almost think that it was nothing else than a revival of the old Wobbly song: the Movement was an attempt to bridge the gap between what America in actual fact was and what it should or could have been. But the peculiar spell of *The Crying of Lot 49* comes from the fact that – however Pynchon might have felt at the time – the book acutely registers the fascination exerted by the other, "religious" (as opposed to "political") interpretation of the Tristero's "otherness."[61] The two alternatives are here kept open: the Tristero as an utterly "other" order whose intrusion into this world will "turn the world upside down" and spell sheer terror, and the Tristero as a new tryst with a long-forgotten America.

This not only makes *The Crying of Lot 49* truer to the "topical" mood of the times than *Vineland's* later nostalgic reconstruction of the 1960s via the 1980s, but also brings it in line with an American tradition going back to the "declension" sermons of the seventeenth century. This short novel has a long background; and to quote from *Vineland,* a vast "hinterland of time" stretches somberly here "from the honkey-tonk coast of Now."[62] Although it is from a topical point of view a novel of 1957–1964, enclosed in it, Borges fashion, one finds a whole micro-encyclopedia of past historical events. The Tristero, as the "excluded" third Oedipa becomes aware of – the "third" world ignored by official America – partly derives from the "Orbis Tertius" of the first "Encyclopedia of Tlön" in Borges's story "Tlön, Uqbar, Orbis Tertius." Like the Tristero conspiracy (although somewhat later), the "Encyclopedia of Tlön" begins when a "persecuted brotherhood" decides to invent from scratch another land which, after a long interval of silence and secrecy, resurfaces – again like the Tristero – in nineteenth-century North America and starts intruding "clues" into the real world.[63] The patient reconstruction of the Tristero goes back to the early beginnings of the Thurn and Taxis postal system (in Bergamo around 1290), but the main focus is on the period of the Thirty

Years' War (1616–48), the war which dislocated the old imperial map of Europe. These were the critical years for the Thurn and Taxis postal system: as each nation started establishing its own postal system, its empire shrank to a little more than a ghost of its former self. Fences, as it were, went up everywhere in what had once been an imperial "zone," the Old World's counterpart of the American wilderness.

The outbreak of the Thirty Years' War also marks the moment when in Jacobean England the process of revolution began. This eventually resulted both in the exodus (before the threatened catastrophe) of a holy remnant to the New World, there to plant a "Lord's Plantation," and in the dark outburst of violence of the "saints in arms" leading to a civil war in England – both historical phenomena blooming from the same seed, twin efflorescences of the same root.[64] In historical terms, the "49" of the novel's title might be construed to refer to 1849, when ("forty-niners" of sorts) the Tristero came to America in the wake of the failure of the 1848 European revolutions (and came at the wrong time, when the U.S. government, as part of its "headlong expansion" into the West, was erecting legal fences in the newly conquered "wilderness," thus reenacting for this incarnation of "shadowy Trystero" the same pattern of eviction the original had already gone through). But the "49" may also refer to 1649, the year that John Winthrop, governor of the "Lord's Plantation of Massachusetts Bay," died, and the "awful hieroglyph" of *The Scarlet Letter* flashed on the New England sky.[65] It was also the peak year of the revolution in England; the year King Charles I was led to the scaffold and beheaded; the year the Levellers' manifesto was published; and the year Gerrard Winstanley took the lead in establishing a Digger colony in Sussex, to reclaim the "waste" England had become and return it to the poor and downtrodden.[66] Chronologically, then, Jacobean 1618 is the first "threshold" in the book, with its "landscape of evil Richard Wharfinger had fashioned for his 17th-century audiences, so preapocalyptic, death-wishful, sensually fatigued, unprepared a little poignantly for the abyss of civil war that had been waiting, cold and deep, only a few years ahead of them" (65). Beyond that threshold, the world is either to collapse into destruction or to bloom into a new world – or, in a variant on

Pynchon's trope, simultaneously to implode and to explode. On a much larger scale, *Gravity's Rainbow* will exploit the same twofold structure as a novel of 1969, the year when America both collapsed inward and nearly vanished into the black hole – "the world's asshole" – of Vietnam and voyaged outward on an exploring trek to the moon and ultimately beyond.

For Pynchon, this historical compression is also "personal." *Gravity's Rainbow* will later make clear how highly conscious Pynchon is of his "conspicuous pedigree" (to use Henry James's phrase about Hawthorne), tracing Slothrop's ancestry all the way back to the original Slothrop who came to America as a cook aboard Governor's Winthrop's flagship, the *Arbella*. He is of that lineage of American writers who, from Hawthorne through Emily Dickinson, Henry Adams, T. S. Eliot and Robert Lowell down to William Gaddis, have felt American history in their bones and could recount it from the annals of their own families. The kinship with Hawthorne goes fairly deep. Just as Hawthorne's family, after its first glory, gradually "sunk almost out of sight," the House of Pynchon somewhere along the line lapsed from its "quondam glory" into obscurity.[67] When Pynchon – like so many American writers before him – comes to write what might be termed (in Sacvan Bercovitch's crucial phrase) "a national biography," he writes it, as it were, from the point of view of his shadowy twin, as if he had been not Pynchon but Thomas Maule all the time, evicted from his rightful legacy and actually disinherited. "Last of his line and how far fallen" (Slothrop's phrase about himself in *Gravity's Rainbow*), Pynchon – again like Hawthorne – might have lapsed from his ancestry by becoming "a scribbler of bygone days" and a "fiddler" of sorts (or at least a kazoo player). But his ancestry varies from Hawthorne's in two important ways. First, William Pynchon – the founder of Springfield – came to America as part of the 1630 Winthrop fleet. Second, William Pynchon found himself at one point on the wrong side of the hedge, when on October 10, 1650, the General Court ordered that his pamphlet "The Meritorious Price of our Redemption" be burned in the Market Place at Boston because of the doctrinal aberrations, errors and heresies it contained.[68] He can thus – whatever the actual historical record – be construed as the other Winthrop, his shadowy twin. By analogy, the Pynchon family's lapse into obscurity can be viewed as an emblem of the way America has betrayed its original "errand" into the wilderness when the "Win/throp" thrust toward headlong conquest, land grabbing, exploitation and destruction suppressed and forced underground, to the edge of utter oblivion and extinction, the opposite "slothropism" that seeks to merge with the land. As a reader of William Carlos Williams's *In the American Grain*, Pynchon feels a compulsion to expose and indict the Puritan legacy and imprint, but he does so on behalf of and in the name of not De Soto or Daniel Boone, but an original Puritan settler, a shadow-image of the first governor of the Bay Colony. This is to recognize the counter-history of America, difficult at times to distinguish from the official version, and more accurately a ghostly double of it, just as the Tristero is both official and subversive.

Moving from history to figure, we have seen that, lured out of her enclosure, Oedipa ventures across the tracks, into the wilderness without. But one should here also underline how information theory revives and rephrases the age-old dual and paradoxical construction of the "wilderness" reflected throughout seventeenth-century sermons, captivity narratives, and scriptural allusion. The "wilderness" there is the "waste howling wilderness" of Deuteronomy. The Plantation is the Lord's walled-in enclosure, his enclosed garden (the "hortus conclusus" of The Song of Solomon). Outside this "clearing" is the "wilderness" where land is not enclosed or cultivated, but left to lie waste. This forlorn waste land is the emblem of man's spiritual estrangement from God. Should the Lord uproot his hedge, his vineyard would lapse back to that waste, a place of ruins, decay and dead bones, weeds and sand. But the "wilderness" is also the place into which one escapes to hear the Lord's dispensation, where one can hear his voice – not garbled or distorted by human inventions and admixtures, but clearly, the place one goes to wait for the descent of the New Jerusalem, a place of religious insight. Venturing into the wilderness in the figures deployed by scores of Colonial sermons and narratives, one is exposed both to wild chaos and to a new revelation.

Similarly, information theory suggests that utter randomness can be seen from two perspectives. In the breakdown of all order, everything lapses back into entropic chaos; but at the same time the odds are that, from this random chaos, a radically new, utterly "original" informational order will arise. W.A.S.T.E. can then be read as "We Await Silent Tristero's Empire" – as the expectation of this new order, rather than just detritus or noise. Walking across the tracks into Tristero territory, Oedipa feels she is to become an outcast, but in her newfound exile, she has that final vision where she makes exactly the same sort of imaginative leaps that the sermons I am here summarizing characteristically make. American has devolved from its "quondam glory" – from the glory that once was or might have been. As Oedipa follows the other outcasts in their "withdrawal" from the Republic, she finds a Kingdom within and has, in her way, what Puritanism called "a Glimpse of Sion's Glory."[69]

Oedipa is eventually restored to the wilderness condition that was America's primeval condition and is thus enabled to recapture its lost origin, beyond the fork where the wrong path was taken. In *The Crying of Lot 49*, the wilderness as waste is inhabited by all sorts of entropic drifters – bums, hoboes, transients, vagrants, derelicts, all "written off." They are, as we have seen, outside the enclosure, cast out into its shadowy margins. They seem, like the Tristero, to have "withdrawn" from the Republic. But they have withdrawn in much the same way that, in declension sermons, the Lord was so often said to have withdrawn from New England. The Kingdom that Oedipa feels is about to come in the auction room of the novel's final scenes is "another" kingdom, and yet, at the same time, it is nothing but "America" itself – not the official America of barbed-wire enclosures or high-security perimeters that has super-imposed its grid upon the forlorn land, but the "America" promised, the America that once was, "the only true America" – waiting to be redeemed from its captivity. At the end of the story, she is expecting in more than one sense. Just as the hidden, other America is about to be delivered from her long "captivity" among specters and shadows, Oedipa, delivered from her virginal self-encapsulation to become a "pierced" Pietà/Christ, is now about to be "delivered" of what the "logos spermatikos" has impregnated her with. The Other world about to be revealed to her is also about to be brought forth through her, to be born out of her. The "interim," in-between, time and space turns out to be a version of the Joy-cean "uterim" as another, alternative world which has been all the time in gestation, figuratively, within her. She is "pregnant" with something "[y]our gynecologist has no test for" (175). Call it America, but America both as waste land and as vineyard, such as it was at the origin and will again be at the novel's consummation of time, now approaching fast.

Compared to *Vineland*, which bears resemblances to *The Crying of Lot 49* in its envisioning of "America," one notes the "compression" here – both violent destruction and total redemption are awaited at the same time. This paradox, I have tried to show, reflects both the mood of the sixties and the contradictory view of the wilderness that figured in the literature of the Puritans. In other terms, the Tristero about to be revealed is both "the submerged fifth" (as the Wobblies used to say) to be gathered back into the American fold as America closes the gap between what it is and what it should have been – a return of the vanishing America keeping a tryst with its original promise – and a "Fifth Monarchy," arising to wreck havoc and sheer terror, ushering in the new dispensation. *The Crying of Lot 49* suggests that it could go either way, as Oedipa awaits, in the end, what in seventeenth-century parlance could be called an "awful Nativity."

The Last Delta-T

Hovering in the background of *The Crying of Lot 49* is the ghost of the old eschatological plot (call it "plot 49") which – perhaps since well before a "holy remnant" sailed on the *Arbella* to the New World, just in time to escape destruction, but certainly at least since the seventeenth century in America and down through *Moby Dick, The Scarlet Letter,* and *The Narrative of A. Gordon Pym* – has been the canonical plot of American fiction: the unfolding of a story through a suspended time which, paradoxically, rushes toward its own end. In Pynchon, we are always in "the final days," and time is only whatever time is left; the countdown toward zero, which has already started, can always be heard ticking away. The signs one scrutinizes and deciphers are the Biblical "semeia ton kairon" – signs and symptoms of the forthcoming violent irruption of the sacred into this world. The Endzeit is at hand and will recapture the Urzeit. "At midnight" there will be "a cry": "Behold, the bridegroom comes" (Matthew 25:6), the "cry that might," in a "flash," "abolish the night" (118). Then those who remain shall no more see "through a glass, darkly" (I Corinthians 13:12), but face to face shall be exposed to what *Gravity's Rainbow* will call the Kirghiz Light, when "the face of God is a presence," "in the time of the final days."[70] In Pynchon's apocalypse, they shall know no more "in part" (I Corinthians 13:12), nor be any longer, as is Oedipa at the start of her quest, "faced with a metaphor of God knew how many parts" (109), but everything will be "blindingly connected" into One, whereas "on Margate Sands. / I can connect / Nothing with nothing."[71] Oedipa has been "pierced" a first time, and the Word through her has been made flesh (as the plot has been fleshed out), but this is only one moment in its unfolding. She is now waiting for the "other moment" that T. S. Eliot refers to when he writes: "This is a moment, but know that another shall pierce you with sudden joy when the figure of God's purpose is made complete."[72] In the novel, she is nearing the famous point described in *Four Quartets:* perhaps not exactly the "point of intersection of the timeless with time," but at least, through the "hints and guesses" that inundate her, the first foreshadowing of a recognition.[73]

This would seem, at first glance, to be close to the modernist credo that although we live among hints, guesses and cryptic clues, like so many "fragments" we shore against our ruins, there is still the "center" – lost, but to be regained. When, in the end, the ultimate (dis)closure comes, that center will be restored as the origin. In-between time and space will collapse; wasted time and waste land will be at last redeemed. Signs and words – the symptoms of our fallen condition – will be revivified by the living voice; the "shadow" will no longer fall. But in order to place Pynchon in relation to T. S. Eliot's modernism, it is necessary to refer to the missing link in that connection, the other major post-Beat cum post-Eliot American novel, *The Recognitions* by William Gaddis. Gaddis, in the character of his protagonist, Wyatt Gwyon, still wants to detect and "recognize" in each fallen fragment at least the shadow of the origin(al): "not invention but sense of recall, recognition, patterns already there."[74] When, like a defeated Orpheus, he fails in that "recognition" of the original voice, seeing everywhere nothing but "counterfeits" – the saints being "counterfeits" of Christ, who is himself but a counterfeit of God – his disappointed hope turns into a savage indictment of the entropic babble of the waste land. Wyatt's quest still reflects the Eliotian stance, but darkly turned upside down – no longer in the hope of regaining the lost center, but despairing at its irredeemable eclipse.

The ghost of that "plot" still exists in Pynchon, but it has become little more than a ghost. The overall scheme of Pynchon's narrative – both in *The Crying of Lot 49* and in *Gravity's Rainbow* – is that of a symptomatic approach to a "holy center." In some sense, both novels would seem at first glance to be closed structures, rounding out the world as a redeemed whole. As in the "riverrun" of *Finnegan's Wake,* in their end is their beginning: at the end of *The Crying of Lot 49,* Oedipa awaits "the crying of lot 49," bringing us back full circle to the title. But this "closure" in Pynchon is both an optical illusion and a lure. Should one get back to that lost center and recover the lost Aleph, one would be swallowed up into its black hole, as is suggested by the ominous darkness of the novel's closed auction room: closure here amounts to a gravitational collapse, while on the other side of that maelstrom, the implosion becomes an explosion which scatters the world again into the fragments of an endless *"opera aperta."*

It is important to note that, in *The Crying of Lot 49,* the approach of the "center" is asymptotic. Oedipa is "at the edge of . . . the voluptuous field" (118) where the living cry might burst out. She is separated from this "holy center" only by a "vanishingly small instant" (129) when the gap between clues and signs and the Word will at last be closed. But it never will be, and the "time differential" will defer forever the expected end. By one of those temporal coincidences that fill Pynchon's fiction, with the recognition of this temporal gap ever deferring the manifestation of the "center," we might feel that we are "not in Kansas anymore," but rather entering Derrida country. *The Crying of Lot 49* was published in March 1966 and – signs of the times – in the fall of the same year Derrida gave at Johns Hopkins University his seminal lecture exposing the "center" as the ghost still haunting the modernist–

structuralist dream of the word as a "verbal icon" and the old plot that would, by anticipating the end, revive the origin.[75] This is not, of course, to imply that Pynchon read Derrida, or the other way around (despite this writer's insistence that he should), but they share − in a way that neither Eliot nor Gaddis did − a "postmodernist" insight.[76] This insight can be put in terms of Derrida's sense of Joycean temporality: of the two twins struggling for mastery in *Finnegans Wake,* Shem the Penman and Shaun the Postman, Shaun the Postman was quite possibly born first, forever "already there" by the time Shem comes on the scene: at the beginning was the "Post," the temporary aftermath.[77] Signs and words (says the shadow of the old plot) keep us from revelation. Pynchon's novels take place on that border where "words are only an eye-twitch away from the things they stand for" and where one can feel − *tremendum et fascinans* − the awful presence of the unutterable name.[78]

"Intimations of a truer kingdom," except that "no Sunday afternoon Agfa plate could ever bear" that "charismatic flash," and as she approaches "the edge of revelation" Oedipa is aware that words are there also to protect her from glory or redemption, "or whatever it is the word is there, buffering, to protect us from" (129).[79] So that, as regards the central "revelation," the "postmodern" strategy is both to approach and to avoid it. Words keep us in exile from our home, they prevent the revelation of the Kingdom: "We are in exile, but we do have a home. A messenger from the kingdom is arriving at the last moment," like the descending angel in the last split second of the novel, but he keeps coming and never arrives; this is "the end," but history is made up of "ends" − it is a "closure without end, an end without end."[80]

The peculiar American note in Pynchon is the buoyancy this deferred end gives to the whole venture of writing. God, wrote Emily Dickinson, refuses to loosen the Seal of Revelation; instead, he inflicts "the Seal Despair," the trauma that leaves no physical scars, "but internal difference / Where the Meanings are."[81] The apocalyptic scenario is foregrounded in Pynchon's text as we move toward the point at which "something in us must leap and sing, or withdraw in fright" − the twofold aspect of the apocalypse, as well as of the Tristero, as redemption or destruction, Day of Glory or Day of Wrath — but expressed here as a self-conscious fiction.[82] God is as dead for Pynchon as for many other modern writers, but, reading his work, we still wait for and approach that "point" outside and beyond the text, though Pynchon makes us fully aware that this is a fictional construct. The tone of awe surrounding Oedipa's approach toward an "advent" almost drowns out Pynchon's other note — the jubilation felt at the discovery that, in the last split second before closure (the first of many last split seconds), we can play with signs and words and invent worlds upon worlds. There are so many self-conscious echoes of T. S. Eliot in Pynchon that one is apt to forget the other strain to which he, more deeply perhaps, belongs (in shorthand, the Emerson–Whitman–Stevens line). As the last delta-t rushes us forever to the end, it renews each time our freedom to go on projecting words upon what is to become a blank world. The gap is about to close, but "in the meantime" we still have a chance of weaving words and so to find a home — not in any lost center from which we would have been exiled, but in the very filling of that endless, fortunate gap.

Post-Script: da capo

The End, then. And yet, once one has come full circle, as it were, and construed the book as a "metaphysical" (in the seventeenth-century sense of the word) emblem of the whole of American literature, once one has "closed" it, in more ways than one, there is that aftermath — a lingering echo which will not fade into oblivion. An intricate metaphysical artifact *The Crying of Lot 49* certainly is, but — not unlike a John Donne poem — the crucial thing about this micro-encyclopedia is less its construction than its lyrical thrust: its particular "voice print," what one might call Pynchon's "blue note." Any "blue note" is notoriously hard to capture, but one may make a clumsy attempt anyway. The book, as noted above, closes on the phrase "Oedipa settled back, to await the crying of lot 49" (183). But "the crying of lot 49" being the title, this also means that, in a way, the book ends, or stops short, on the suspended closure of the word "await": as in *Gravity's Rainbow*, "[s]omething is going to happen, and you can only wait."[83] Oedipa who, early in the novel, takes the role of a frantic decipherer looking for the lost key to the scribble, learns, as clues and signs keep multiplying, "not to ask questions any more": "Even a month ago, Oedipa's next question would have been 'why?'. But now she kept a silence, waiting, as if to be illuminated" (152). Waiting is the keynote of the book, and as Oedipa has by the end drifted far away from what was once her world, she speculates that "perhaps she'd be hounded someday as far as joining Tristero itself, if it existed, in its twilight, its aloofness, its waiting. The waiting above all" (181).

One feels throughout the novel how much the eschatological scheme haunting the story like a ghost accompanies a sexual crescendo, slowly building up until one reaches the cliff-edge, the archetype in a way of the "liminal situation." In Eliot as well, one remembers, there was "no end to the voiceless waiting," but the waiting itself is different in Pynchon. Here one does not attempt to rush across that gap in order to speed up the coming of the Lord, but rather to protract that last moment – to make it unending, or at least endlessly repeated, like a movie's last shot projected again and again on a screen. One actually feels less the tragically hurried urgency of the countdown to zero (although it is there, of course, as a kind of undertone without which there would be no thrill) than the awful voluptuousness of the waiting – holding it right there, on this limen. Compared again to Eliot, the waiting in Pynchon, although it appears to speed up time and usher in the Apocalypse, in actual fact rather opens up – in a Rilkean sense – space. Whoever is "rushing closer" at the end of *The Crying of Lot 49*, whatever face He that comes – "*o erkhomenos*" – will prove to have, the Advent will also take us, like Rilke's Angel, "ins Freie," into open space. This near-coming is awe-ful, and *Gravity's Rainbow* will describe exactly how it feels, "coming awake in the very late night, blinking up into painful daylight, waiting for the annihilation, the blows from the sky, drawn terribly tense with the waiting, unable to name whatever is approaching . . . *Erwartung* in the cross-hairs, with the just-sprung rye blowing."[84] *Gravity's Rainbow* will also make much more explicit the connection between eschatological and sexual expectation ("Far from rag, snow, lacerated streets, she huddles here in the Asian dust with her buttocks arched skyward, awaiting the first touch of him – of it")

161

but the connection is there in *The Crying of Lot 49* as a haunting undertone.[85] The expected "cry" has not come yet, and meanwhile, in the mean time, what we have in Pynchon is a hum, a "hushed expectancy." In the last lull before the cry becomes the "scream" that "comes" across the sky, a lullaby is hummed on lower frequencies. The Puritan score originally written, in the seventeenth century, by Samuel Danforth and Increase Mather, comes finally to be played by, from across the tracks, Bird on his magic horn, or by Monk on his ghostly piano.[86] And perhaps reading Pynchon ultimately means (once the semiotic shenanigans are over and done with) remaining alert to that particular voice's print and listening, "in hushed expectancy," not only to the words, but to the lull in between, and to the "hum," out there.

NOTES

1. If we are to believe Jules Siegel: "He [Pynchon] felt that he had rushed through *The Crying of Lot 49* in order to get the money. He was taking no such chance with the new book, apparently having begun it soon after the publication of *V.*, interrupting it to write *The Crying of Lot 49*." See Siegel's "Who is Thomas Pynchon . . . And Why Did He Take Off with My Wife?", *Playboy* (March 1977): 171. What happened to *The Crying of Lot 49* is all the odder as Pynchon keeps dismissing it. Thus, in the "Introduction" to *Slow Learner*: "The next story I wrote was "The Crying of Lot 49," which was marketed as a 'novel,' and in which I seem to have forgotten most of what I'd learned up till then." Thomas Pynchon, *Slow Learner: Early Stories* (Boston: Little, Brown, 1984), p. 22.

2. Timothy Leary, Ralph Metzner, and Richard Alpert, *The Psychedelic Experience: A Manual Based on the Tibetan Book of the Dead* (New Hyde Park, N.Y.: University Books, 1964).

3. Timothy Leary, *Flashbacks: An Autobiography* (Los Angeles: J. P. Tarcher, 1983), p. 253.

4. Note these lines from *The Crying of Lot 49*: "The act of metaphor then was a thrust at truth and a lie, depending where you were: inside, safe, or outside, lost. Oedipa did not know where she was. Trembling, unfurrowed, she slipped sidewise, screeching back across grooves of

years" (p. 129). Unfurrowed, delirious ("lira" being in Latin a "fur-row" or "groove"), not only is Oedipa topically "groovy," but coming off her groove, she finds her way, as I will argue, back to the oldest furrow in American culture.

5. "Osberg" was Nabokov's fond name for Borges.
6. Brian Stonehill has brilliantly commented on some of the similarities between the two books in "On Harry Matthews," *Chicago Review* 33, 2 (1982): 107.
7. "We are at a transition point, a strange post-Beat passage of cultural time, with our loyalties divided. As bop and rock 'n roll were to swing music and postwar pop, so was this new writing [then being pub-lished in the *Evergreen Review*] to the most established modernist tra-dition we were being exposed to in college." Thomas Pynchon, "In-troduction" to *Slow Learner*, p. 9.
8. Jack Kerouac, *On the Road* (London: Penguin, 1972), p. 13.
9. Chandler Brossard will use this phrase for the title of his Beat novel, *Who Walk in Darkness*; the second phrase comes from T. S. Eliot, "Ash Wednesday," in *Selected Poems* (London: Faber and Faber, 1954): 90.
10. Thomas Pynchon, "Introduction" to *Slow Learner*, p. 7.
11. Caroline Bird, "Born 1930: The Unlost Generation," *Harper's Bazaar* (February 1957). The Tristero, whatever kinship it will finally seem to have with the underground church of the Catacombs, is at first very close to what Howard S. Becker (mentioned in the article) describes as a "subculture of marginal men." "The White Negro" was first published in *Dissent* in 1957; the essay has been collected in *Advertisements for Myself* (London: Corgi, 1963), where Mailer pre-sents it as "the real end of this muted autobiography of the near-beat adventurer who was myself" (p. 241).
12. "Horny Anonymous," as Pynchon will put it more straightforwardly in *Gravity's Rainbow* (New York: Viking, 1983), p. 547.
13. Thomas Pynchon, "Introduction" to *Slow Learner*, p. 8.
14. Thomas Pynchon, "The Secret Integration" (first published in *The Saturday Evening Post*, December 1964), in *Slow Learner*, p. 179.
15. Ralph Ellison, *Invisible Man* (1952; rpt. New York: Vintage, 1980), p. 440; my emphases.
16. Thomas Pynchon, *Gravity's Rainbow*, p. 681.
17. The passage from Eliot's "Ash Wednesday" reads: "Will the veiled sister pray for / Those who walk in darkness, who chose thee and oppose thee, / Those who are torn on the horn between season and season, time and time, between / Hour and hour, word and word,

power and power, those who wait / In darkness?" T. S. Eliot, *Selected Poems*, p. 90.

18. J. D. Salinger, *The Catcher in the Rye* (London: Penguin, 1951), p. 124. Pynchon's version of the same perception can be found in his comments on "Entropy":

What strikes me nowadays about the story is not so much its thermodynamic gloom as the way it reflects how the '50's were for some folks. I suppose it is as close to a Beat story as anything I was writing then, although I thought I was sophisticating the Beat spirit with second-hand science. I wrote "Entropy" in '58 or '59 – when I talk about '57 in the story as "back then" I am being almost sarcastic. One year of those times was much like another. One of the most pernicious effects of the '50's was to convince the people growing up during them that it would last forever. Until John Kennedy, then perceived as a congressional haircut with a strange haircult, began to get some attention, there was a lot of aimlessness going on. While Eisenhower was in, there seemed to be no reason why it should all not just go on as it was. ("Introduction" to *Slow Learner*, p. 14)

19. As was the case for many, Thomas Pynchon probably first heard about information theory from reading Norbert Weiner's *The Human Use of Human Beings*, a book written in 1949 which brought out the relevance of Weaver's and Shannon's scientific theory in terms of the political climate of the times; Weiner argued that there is no way one can protect information by locking it up in an enclosure as it undergoes entropical decay. It is nice to speculate that Pynchon was aware of the most widely read book on information theory, *Symbols, Signals and Noise: The Nature and Process of Communication* (New York: Harper, 1961) by, as it turns out, J. R. Pierce. More important, perhaps, 1957–64 was the time when information theory was making its first inroads into aesthetic and literary analysis, with the work of Abraham Moles and with Umberto Eco's *Opera Aperta*, which Eco began in 1958 and eventually published in 1962, which concerns the same time-span as *The Crying of Lot 49* and which partakes of the trend moving from closure to openness.

20. Among the symbolic potentials of the "I/O" configuration is that of the erect "I" standing for phallic closure and "O" for openness, crossroads, and "diversity of chances." This kind of hieroglyphic reading will achieve its full scope in *Gravity's Rainbow*.

21. The story was published in *Esquire* under the title "The World (This One), The Flesh (Mrs. Oedipa Maas) and the Testament of Pierce Inverarity," *Esquire* (December 1965): 170–73, 196. The title rang a bell for any French reader. Our literature is not notably rich in Protestant poetry, but the masterpiece of the genre is probably Jean de

Sponde's "Sonnet XII," where he lists the three things that tempt him and threaten the interior realization of "God's Temple": "Tout s'enfle contre moy, tout m'assault et me tente et le monde [the World], et la chair [the Flesh], et l'Ange revolt [the rebellious Angel]."

22. One finds here a first sketchy delineation of what will eventually become a major theme in Pynchon. *Gravity's Rainbow* takes place in the same twilight "zone" which Jean Cocteau, in *Le Testament d'Orphée*, one of the movies being shown at the Orpheus Theater in the final pages of the novel, described thus: "La vie est longue tre morte; ce'st la Zone" ("life takes a long time dying; it's the Zone"). The Shade Creek episodes of *Vineland* will further develop this idea: "The soul newly in transition doesn't like to admit — indeed will deny quite vehemently — that it's really dead" (Thomas Pynchon, *Vineland* [Boston: Little, Brown, 1989], p. 228). In *Vineland* the sense of expectation has almost faded away, but not in *The Crying of Lot 49*, where the ghostly inhabitants of the "zone" are both after-images of a world gone and fore-shadows of a world to come.

23. Cf. Arnold Van Gennep, *Les Rites de passage* (Paris: Nourry, 1909).

24. "Passerino," in Italian, is a little sparrow, the "birdie" about to come out of the camera and to print in a flash the Agfa plate; but it is also a fond nickname for the penis. In a characteristic compounding of senses, Oedipa is about to be "pierced" by a coming revelation.

25. On the significance of the threshold in American literature, see Edwin Fussell, *Frontier: American Literature and the American West* (Princeton: Princeton University Press, 1965), and Frederick Garber, *Thoreau's Redemptive Imagination* (New York: New York University Press, 1977).

26. *Vineland*, p. 228.

27. Tony Tanner, *The Reign of Wonder: Naivety and Reality in American Literature* (Cambridge University Press, 1965), p. 274.

28. The particular references here are to Henry James, *The Wings of the Dove* (London: Penguin, 1965), pp. 145, 134, 292.

29. Henry James, *The Art of the Novel* (New York: Scribner's, 1934), p. 256.

30. The "pierced aperture" is part of James's famous figure of "the house of fiction" depicted in the "Preface" to *The Portrait of A Lady* (1908; rpt. New York: Houghton Mifflin, 1963), p. 7.

31. Henry James, "Preface" to *The Princess Casamassima*, in *The Art of the Novel*, p. 76.

32. Ibid., p. 77.

33. Henry James, *The Ambassadors* (1903; rpt. New York: W. W. Norton, 1964), p. 20.

34. Gleaning *The Wings of the Dove*, for instance, one finds "the odd part was" (p. 197), "the result was the oddest consciousness of" (p. 144), or "it will give an oddity to my silence" (p. 277).

35. Thomas Pynchon, *Gravity's Rainbow*, p. 85.

36. Henry James, *The Ambassadors*, p. 313.

37. Ibid.

38. Henry James, *The Wings of the Dove*, p. 476.

39. Thomas Pynchon, *Vineland*, p. 226. The use of "revelation" both in its eschatological and its chemical (photographic) sense is a favorite trope of Pynchon's.

40. "Among them" [James Forrester, John Foster Dulles, and Senator Joseph McCarthy], "those dear daft numina who'd mothered over Oedipa's so temperate youth had managed to turn young Oedipa into a rare creature indeed, unfit perhaps for marches and sit-ins, but just a whiz at pursuing strange words in Jacobean texts" (p. 104).

41. See Pynchon's "A Journey into the Mind of Watts," *New York Times Magazine* (12 June 1966): 34–5, 78, 80–2, 84.

42. From Nerval: "Je suis le ténébreux, le veuf, l'inconsolé / Le Prince d'Aquitaine à la tour abolie, / Ma seule étoile est morte, et mon luth constellé, / Porte le soleil noir de la mélancholie."

43. From Rilke's seventh *Duino Elegy*: "Jeder dumpfe Umkehr des Welt hat solce Enterbte, / Denen das Fruhere nicht und noch nicht das Nachste gehrt."

44. "Sunt geminae Somni portae, quarum altera fertur / Cornea, qua veris facilis datur exitus umbris" (Virgil). Pynchon may have known these lines, if not directly from Virgil himself, then from Eliot's "Sweeney Among the Nightingales," which alludes to them.

45. "They shall look on Him whom they pierced" (John 19:37). The evidence that Pynchon is aware of these scriptural echoes is re-affirmed in *Gravity's Rainbow*: "Was it really Him, pierced Jesus, who came to lean over you?" (681). Oedipa is potentially both a pierced Jesus being crucified and "pierced" Mary to whom old Simeon says, "Yea, a sword shall pierce through thy own soul also, that the thoughts of many hearts may be revealed" (Luke 2:35).

46. The conflation of these senses of "deliverance" is revealed in this scriptural passage: "O wretched man that I am! Who shall deliver me from the body of this death?" (Rom 7:24).

47. Thomas Pynchon, *Gravity's Rainbow*, p. 3.

48. Richard Brodhead, *Hawthorne, Melville and the Novel* (Chicago: University of Chicago Press, 1976).

49. Jorge Luis Borges, "Baltascar Gracian," in *A Personal Anthology* (London: Picador, 1972), p. 68.

50. Borges, "The Other Tiger," *Personal Anthology*, p. 65.

51. In 1966, Simon and Garfunkel's song "The Sounds of Silence" was at the top of the charts.

52. Walt Whitman, "Song of Myself," lines 85–6, in *Leaves of Grass: Comprehensive Reader's Edition*, ed. Harold W. Blodgett and Sculley Bradley (New York: Norton, 1965), p. 33.

53. Wallace Stevens, *Selected Poems* (London: Faber and Faber, 1963), p. 133.

54. Richard Poirier, "The Embattled Underground," *New York Times Book Review* (1 May 1966): "The whole role given Oedipa makes it impossible to divorce from her limitations the large rhetoric about America at the end of the novel. This is unfortunate simply because Oedipa has not been given character enough to bear the weight of this rhetoric" (p. 42).

55. Speaking in the "Introduction" to *Slow Learner* of the impact of "new writing" (Kerouac, Bellow's *The Adventures of Augie March*), Pynchon comments:

    . . . at least two very distinct kinds of English could be allowed in fiction to coexist. Allowed! It was actually OK to write like this! Who knew? The effect was exciting, liberating, strongly positive. It was not a case of either/or, but an expansion of possibilities. I don't think we were consciously groping after any synthesis, although perhaps we should have been. The success of the "new left" later in the '60's was to be limited by the failure of college kids and blue-collar workers to get together politically. One reason was the presence of real, invisible class force fields in the way of communication between the two groups. (p. 7)

56. As in Leonard Cohen's song, "The Partisan": "Then we'll come from the shadows."

57. Michael Harrington, *The Other America: Poverty in the United States* (London: Penguin, 1963).

58. Harrington, *The Other America*; the passage reads:

    The other America, the America of poverty, is hidden today in a way it never was before. Its millions are socially invisible to the rest of us. . . . Poverty is often off the beaten track. It always has been. The ordinary tourist never left the main highway and today he rides interstate turnpikes . . . They [the poor] have no face, they have no voice . . . They are dispossessed in terms of what the rest of the nation enjoyed, in terms of what the society could provide if it had the will. They live on the fringes, the margin. They watch the movies and read the magazines of affluent America and these tell them that they are internal exiles. (pp. 101–103)

59. As far as we can gather from a few scattered clues, Pynchon seems to

have been fairly close to Tom Hayden's S.D.S., whose founding Port Huron statement was heavily indebted to Harrington's *The Other America*.

60. See Tom Hayden, *Reunion: A Memoir* (New York: Random House, 1988).
61. A fascination that the short story "Mortality and Mercy in Vienna" – excluded, apparently for copyright reasons, from the *Slow Learner* collection – concisely describes.
62. Pynchon, *Vineland*, p. 180.
63. In Jorge Luis Borges, *Labyrinths* (New York: New Directions, 1964), pp. 3–18.
64. Alan Simpson, in *Puritanism in Old and New England* (Chicago: University of Chicago Press, 1956), has traced how the two branches of Puritanism, originating from the same root, have experienced different fates:

> The first chance to see what the Puritan saint would make of life, if he had the freedom to experiment, came in America. The early history of Massachusetts is the story of men who shared an ideal, left the Old World to realize the New, only to discover that when the work of planting was done the spirit had evaporated. Frustration was the fate that awaited every Puritan. In England, where the defeat came in war, it has all the features of tragedy; here, where there was no defeat but apparent success, it became a kind of ironic tale. (p. 19)

65. In Hawthorne's *The Scarlet Letter,* chapter 12, "The Minister's Vigil":

> It was indeed a majestic idea, that the destiny of nations should be revealed in these awful hieroglyphs, on the cope of the heavens. A scroll so wide might not be deemed too expansive for Providence to write a people's doom upon . . . the minister, looking upward to the zenith, beheld there the appearance of an immense letter – the letter A – marked out in lines of dull red light." (Nathaniel Hawthorne, *The Scarlet Letter* [London: Penguin, 1970], pp. 174–5)

66. *The True Levellers Standard Advanced* (London, 1649). Since in Thomas Pynchon's world everything holds (historically) together, this seemingly distant connection should not be considered mere idle and speculative scholarship. The troubled sixties saw a marked revival of interest in the English Puritan Revolution, particularly in its more radical aspects. In 1966 – the same year as *The Crying of Lot 49* was published – came the first book to investigate in depth the "lunatic fringe" of the Puritan Movement, P. G. Rogers, *The Fifth Monarchy Men* (London: Oxford University Press, 1966). Meanwhile, in California, Emmett Grogan [Kenny Wisdom] of *Ringolevio* fame was calling his militant group "the Diggers" in a twofold reference to the Nevada Indians and to Winstanley.

67. Nathaniel Hawthorne, "The Custom House," in *The Scarlet Letter*, p. 42.

68. On William Pynchon, see Samuel Eliot Morison, *Builders of the Bay Colony* (New York: Houghton Mifflin, 1962), and Philip F. Gura, *A Glimpse of Sion's Glory: Puritan Radicalism in New England 1620–1660* (Middletown, Conn.: Wesleyan University Press, 1986).

69. "If there be many Prophesies and Promises in Scripture that are not yet fulfilled, the fulfilling whereof will bring the Church into a more glorious condition than ever it was yet in the world: then there is a glorious Time coming. . . . The nearer the Time comes, the more clearly these things shall be revealed. And because they begin to be revealed so much as they doe now, we have cause to know that Time is at hand." Thomas Goodwin, *A Glimpse of Syon's Glory* (1641), quoted by Gura, *A Glimpse*, p. 2.

70. Pynchon, *Gravity's Rainbow*, p. 358.

71. T. S. Eliot, *The Waste Land*, lines 300–302, in *Collected Poems 1909–1962* (New York: Harcourt, Brace & World, 1970), p. 64.

72. T. S. Eliot, *Murder in the Cathedral* (New York: Harcourt, Brace & World, 1963), p. 69.

73. T. S. Eliot, *Four Quartets*, "The Dry Salvages," lines 210–220, in *Collected Poems*, pp. 198–9.

74. William Gaddis, *The Recognitions* (New York: Harcourt, Brace & Co., 1955; rpt. with corrections, Cleveland and New York: World Publishing Company, 1962), p. 123.

75. Jacques Derrida, "Structure, Sign and Play in the Discourse of Human Science," in his *Writing and Difference*, trans. Alan Bass (Chicago: University of Chicago Press, 1976).

76. I do not know if Derrida has read Pynchon; perhaps he has. But in any case, it is rather fascinating to speculate on the fact that *The Crying of Lot 49* is, after all, about "couriers" and contains, among other wonders, a micro-history of postal delivery in the Western world, which is exactly what Derrida was later to say he had always dreamed of writing and what he would sketch out in *La Carte Postale* (Paris: Flammarion, 1980).

77. "Au commencement, en principe, tait la poste, et je ne m'en consolerai jamais." Derrida, *La Carte Postale*, p. 34.

78. Thomas Pynchon, *Gravity's Rainbow*, p. 100.

79. Ibid., p. 579.

80. Jacques Derrida, "Of an Apocalyptic Tone Recently Adopted in Philosophy," trans. John P. Leavey, Jr., *Semia* 23 (1982): 95.

81. Emily Dickinson, #248 ("There's a certain slant of light"), *Selected*

Poems and Letters of Emily Dickinson, ed. Robert N. Linscott (New York: Doubleday, 1959), p. 74.

82. Ibid., p. 396.
83. Ibid., p. 122.
84. Ibid., p. 343.
85. Ibid.
86. I refer here to Samuel Danforth's *A Brief Recognition of New England's Errand into the Wilderness* (1670), and to the jazz music of Charlie "Bird" Parker and Thelonius Monk.

Notes on Contributors

Debra A. Castillo is Associate Professor of Romance Studies and Comparative Literature at Cornell University. She is the author of *The Translated World: A Postmodern Tour of Libraries in Literature* and of numerous essays on contemporary Latin American, Spanish, and British commonwealth fiction; she is also the editor of *Diacritics*. Her latest project is *Talking Back: Strategies for a Latin American Feminist Literary Criticism*, forthcoming from Cornell University Press.

Bernard Duyfhuizen is Associate Professor of English at the University of Wisconsin–Eau Claire and is one of the editors of *Pynchon Notes*. His book *Narratives of Transmission* will be published in 1992 by Fairleigh Dickinson University Press. His essays have appeared in such journals as *ELH, Novel, Comparative Literature, College English*, and *Modern Fiction Studies*. He is currently at work on a study of Pynchon's use of reader-traps in *Gravity's Rainbow*.

N. Katherine Hayles, Carpenter Professor of English at the University of Iowa, holds advanced degrees in both chemistry and English. Her most recent book is *Chaos Bound: Orderly Disorder in Contemporary Literature and Science*. Currently at work on a project exploring the intersection of discursive and physical constructions of the body in cybernetics, semiotics, and contemporary literature, she spends a lot of time in various virtual realities.

John Johnston is Associate Professor of English and Comparative Literature at Emory University. He is the author of *Carnival of Repetition: Gaddis' The Recognitions and Postmodern Theory* and of many articles on postmodern literature, art, and culture. He is presently completing a book on "chaosmos" and multiplicity in contemporary American fiction.

Patrick O'Donnell, editor of this volume, is the Eberly Family Distinguished Professor of American Literature at West Virginia University. He is the author of *Passionate Doubts: Designs of Interpretation in Contemporary American Fiction;* the co-editor of a collection of essays, *Intertextuality and Contemporary American Fiction;* and an associate editor of the forthcoming *Columbia History of the American Novel.* His most recent book, *Echo Chambers: Figuring Voice in Modern Narrative,* is forthcoming from the University of Iowa Press.

Pierre-Yves Petillon teaches American Literature and American Studies at the École Normale Supérieure in Paris. He is the author of several books and essays on American literature and culture, including *La grande-route: Espace et écriture en Amérique,* a study of the road and the voyage in American literature from Melville to Pynchon. He is currently at work on a number of projects involving historiography, Puritanism, and contemporary American literature.

Selected Bibliography

The edition of *The Crying of Lot 49* used for the purposes of this collection is the 1986 Perennial Library paperback edition (PL 1307), published by Harper and Row in New York: this is the most widely available current reprint. *The Crying of Lot 49* was originally published in 1966 by J. P. Lippincott in Philadelphia; the first British edition of the novel appeared in 1967 and was published by Jonathan Cape of London. Since then, the novel has gone through four paperback reprints: a 1967 Bantam mass market edition, a 1974 Penguin trade edition in Britain, a 1979 Pan trade edition in Britain, and the 1986 Perennial edition. As David Seed notes in "Pynchon's Textual Revisions of *The Crying of Lot 49*," *Pynchon Notes* 12 (June 1983): 39–45, there are minor differences between the portions of the novel published in *Esquire* and *Cavalier* and the Lippincott first edition; Pynchon also made minor (though not wholly insignificant) changes in page proofs that survive in the first edition. But there appear to be very few changes or corrections between the reprints, so that the Perennial Library edition is, for all practical purposes, a straight reprint of the original Lippincott edition.

This selected bibliography cites substantial discussions of *The Crying of Lot 49* contained in book-length considerations of and collections of essays on Pynchon's work; it excludes the considerable body of major Pynchon scholarship which focuses solely on *Gravity's Rainbow*. *Pynchon Notes*, a journal devoted to scholarship and discussion of Pynchon's novels, has published numerous articles on Pynchon in general and on *The Crying of Lot 49* in particular. At present, the definitive bibliography of work by and on Pynchon is Clifford Mead, *Thomas Pynchon: A Bibliography of Primary and Secondary Materials* (Elmwood Park, Ill.: Dalkey Archive Press, 1989).

Bloom, Harold, ed. *Thomas Pynchon: Modern Critical Views*. New York: Chelsea House, 1986.

Colville, Georgianna M. *Beyond and Beneath the Mantle: On Thomas Pynchon's The Crying of Lot 49*. Amsterdam: Rodolpi, 1988.

Cooper, Peter L. *Signs and Symptoms: Thomas Pynchon and the Contemporary World*. Berkeley: University of California Press, 1983.

Cowart, David. *Thomas Pynchon: The Art of Allusion*. Carbondale: Southern Illinois University Press, 1980.

Hite, Molly. *Ideas of Order in the Novels of Thomas Pynchon*. Columbus: Ohio State University Press, 1983.

Ickstadt, Heinz, ed. *Ordnung und Entropie: zum Romanwerk von Thomas Pynchon*. Reinbeck bei Hamburg: Rowohlt, 1981.

Levine, George, and David Leverenz, eds. *Mindful Pleasures: Essays on Thomas Pynchon*. Boston: Little, Brown, 1976.

McConnell, Frank D. *Four Postwar American Novelists: Bellow, Mailer, Barth and Pynchon*. Chicago: University of Chicago Press, 1978.

McHoul, Alec, and David Wills. *Writing Pynchon: Strategies in Fictional Analysis*. Urbana: University of Illinois Press, 1990.

Mendelson, Edward, ed. *Pynchon: A Collection of Critical Essays*. Englewood Cliffs, N.J.: Prentice-Hall, 1978.

Newman, Robert D. *Understanding Thomas Pynchon*. Columbia: University of South Carolina Press, 1986.

Pearce, Richard, ed. *Critical Essays on Thomas Pynchon*. Boston: G. K. Hall, 1981.

Plater, William. *The Grim Phoenix: Reconstructing Thomas Pynchon*. Bloomington: Indiana University Press, 1978.

Schaub, Thomas. *Pynchon: The Voice of Ambiguity*. Urbana: University of Illinois Press, 1980.

Seed, David. *The Fictional Labyrinths of Thomas Pynchon*. Iowa City: University of Iowa Press, 1988.

Slade, Joseph W. *Thomas Pynchon*. New York: Warner Communications, 1974.

Stark, John O. *Pynchon's Fictions: Thomas Pynchon and the Literature of Information*. Athens: Ohio University Press, 1980.

Tanner, Tony. *Thomas Pynchon*. London and New York: Methuen, 1982.